Empowering Lay Volunteers

Creative Leadership Series

Assimilating New Members, Lyle E. Schaller
Beginning a New Pastorate, Robert G. Kemper
The Care and Feeding of Volunteers, Douglas W. Johnson
Creative Stewardship, Richard B. Cunningham
Time Management, Speed B. Leas
Your Church Can Be Healthy, C. Peter Wagner
Leading Churches Through Change, Douglas Alan Walrath
Building an Effective Youth Ministry, Glenn E. Ludwig
Preaching and Worship in the Small Church,
William Willimon and Robert L. Wilson
Church Growth, Donald McGavran and George G. Hunter III
The Pastor's Wife Today, Donna Sinclair
The Small Town Church, Peter J. Surrey
Strengthening the Adult Sunday School Class, Dick Murray
Church Advertising, Steve Dunkin
Women as Pastors, edited by Lyle E. Schaller
Leadership and Conflict, Speed B. Leas
Church Finance in a Complex Economy, Manfred Holck, Jr.
The Tithe, Douglas W. Johnson
Surviving Difficult Church Members, Robert D. Dale
Your Church Has Personality, Kent R. Hunter
The Word on Families, G. William Sheek
Five Audiences, Warren J. Hartman
How to Build a Magnetic Church, Herb Miller
Teaching the Bible to Adults and Youth, Dick Murray
Keys to Building Youth Ministry, Glenn E. Ludwig
The Rural Church, Edward W. Hassinger,
John S. Holik, and J. Kenneth Benson
Clergy and Laity Burnout, William H. Willimon
Direct Mail Ministry, Walter Mueller
Vitality Means Church Growth, Douglas W. Johnson
The Multi-Church Parish, Robert L. Wilson
Six Stages of a Pastor's Life,
J. Keith Cook and Lee C. Moorehead
What Can We Do About Church Dropouts? C. Kirk Hadaway
Empowering Lay Volunteers, Douglas W. Johnson

Empowering Lay Volunteers

Douglas W. Johnson

Creative Leadership Series

Lyle E. Schaller, Editor

Abingdon Press/Nashville

EMPOWERING LAY VOLUNTEERS

Copyright © 1991 by Abingdon Press

Second Printing 1991

This book is printed on recycled, acid-free paper.

Library of Congress Cataloging-in-Publication Data

JOHNSON, DOUGLAS W., 1934–
  Empowering lay volunteers / Douglas W. Johnson.
    p.   cm.—(Creative leadership series)
  ISBN 0-687-11612-0 (alk. paper)
  1. Lay ministry 2. Church workers. I. Title. II. Series.
  BV677.J64   1991
  254'.5—dc20   90-44650

This book is offered to
those dedicated laypersons
who have sought to minister in Christ's
name through the Church. Their name is
Legion and their influence is Eternal.

Foreword

"Maybe we simply should combine our membership committee with the evangelism committee and make them into one committee," suggested a discouraged member of the nominating committee at First Church. "That's how it was in the church we were in before we moved here twelve years ago. Of course, that was a smaller congregation, but I don't see why it wouldn't work here. We're having such a hard time finding people to serve on committees, and that might be a way to reduce the number we need. That way we would have to find only one chairperson, not two, and maybe we could have one large committee with ten people on it, rather than two with seven each. That also would reduce the number of volunteers we need by four and maybe we can finish our job with only one more meeting after this one."

"That's a good idea!" exclaimed another weary member of the nominating committee that was nearing the end of its second meeting, but still had most of its work ahead of it. "I don't see any reason why one committee couldn't handle both sets of responsibilities, and combining the two would make our job easier."

In real life, the proposal to combine these two committees is at best a poor idea. To be more precise, it is a counterproductive action that may represent one component of a larger, unintentional, unarticulated, and unwise design that can be summarized as "the cutback syndrome." This is a remarkably effective strategy for transforming large congregations into middle-sized churches or for shrinking middle-sized congregations into small churches. One component of that strategy is to shrink the number of program committees. A second is to reduce the number of volunteers who are needed. A third component is to assign two different major responsibilities to a single committee. The usual product of such a design is for the committee to neglect one responsibility while concentrating on the other. A fourth component is to formulate policies, such as merging committees, in order to simplify life for leaders. A fifth component is to reduce the number of entry points for new members to serve as volunteers and to earn a sense of belonging. A sixth is to sacrifice quality in order to complete the assignment sooner. Finally, the cutback syndrome is an outstanding example of the self-fulfilling prophecy. We need fourteen volunteers, we reduce the goal to ten, and we declare ourselves to be fortunate to recruit nine. Therefore, reducing the goal from fourteen to ten not only has proved to be a realistic decision, but also has yielded results that demonstrate that we would not have been able to enlist fourteen if we had tried.

This particular nominating committee, described above, is not only a common illustration of the cutback syndrome and an effective strategy for shrinking the size of a congregation, but, even worse, it also is an unchristian and counterproductive approach to enlisting volunteers.

This book introduces a radically different perspective for looking at the role of volunteers in the church. Rather than concentrating on the needs of the institution—including the desire of members of the nominating committee to complete their assignment as quickly and easily as possible—this book focuses on the volunteer. Rather than viewing volunteers as objects to be manipulated, this book begins by listening to the comments of a representative group of potential volunteers. Who are they? What are their needs? How do they view serving as volunteers in the church?

Rather than turning next to the jobs to be filled with warm bodies, the second chapter discusses how people can be motivated to volunteer. The often overlooked distinction between motivation and enlistment is the subject of the third chapter. This chapter is filled with a list of constructive suggestions for facilitating the process of enlistment.

One of the neglected components of a good volunteer system is a healthy, supportive, and productive environment. Volunteers do not function in isolation! The fifth chapter of this book describes how to create and maintain a healthy environment for volunteers. One component is the coordination of volunteers. Another is the volunteer's Bill of Rights. This chapter is essential reading for anyone interested in improving the volunteer system, whether it be in a church or in some other organization.

Time sequence is a critical factor in nurturing a network of volunteers. One aspect of time sequence is considering training *before* giving assignments. The sixth chapter offers dozens of realistic suggestions for training, including the distinction between long-term volunteers and short-term volunteers.

Rather than beginning the seventh chapter, which deals with the topic of assignment, by describing the variety of volunteer responsibilities that exist in most churches, this author reinforces the focus on the volunteer by illustrating how a bad assignment can be an unhappy experience. The last pages of this exceptionally helpful chapter identify eight critical variables in making assignments.

The sensitivity of the author to the needs of volunteers continues through the final two chapters, which discuss rewards, evaluation, termination, and unique situations.

In summary, Dr. Douglas Johnson has made four distinctive contributions in this book. At the top of the list is an examination of the subject from the perspective of the volunteer, rather than from the needs of the institution. Second is the repeated emphasis on the need to create and maintain a healthy environment for volunteers. Third is the scores of clear and specific suggestions for motivating, recruiting, training, placing, and supporting a network of volunteers. Finally, both pastors and volunteer leaders will benefit from the many references to the role of the minister in the care and feeding of the volunteers in your church.

LYLE E. SCHALLER
Yokefellow Institute
Richmond, Indiana

Contents

Preface

This is a new book on volunteers and not a revision of my book *The Care and Feeding of Volunteers*. Since its publication in 1978, the social context has changed and experiences have been added to our understanding of volunteers. Although there are important differences between then and now, much about volunteering remains the same. Thus, this book is written with the feeling that volunteers remain the life and hope of a church.

Diana J. Paulsen, Executive Director, Reformed Church Women, Reformed Church in America, tells of an experience in a strange city at her mother-in-law's wake. Her experience, excerpted from "To the Marys" in *Reformed Review* (Spring 1989), illustrates the kind of impact volunteers have as they express their ministry through service.

The visiting hours were scheduled to begin momentarily. . . . Somewhere in the distance we heard a door open and close. Down the hall came a flurry of noise which abruptly stopped at the entrance to our room. Then they swooped in. . . all seven of them. Who were they? They . . . were

. . . the dispatched representatives of mom's . . . church. They stayed with us all through that first afternoon and gave us their gift of Christian presence as we faced saying goodbye to our mother and to our childhood. . . . These women brought us the gospel.

There are many people like these seven women who want to, and can, help others. This book contains ideas, experiences, and suggestions that can assist churches in equipping such people to be volunteers in ministry.

I

Volunteers—
Who Are They?

A volunteer is a person who provides time and service of her or his own free will. There are no constraints or demands placed on such a person. Time, energy, and effort are given freely. Typically, a volunteer is someone who, upon learning about a need for a person with a specific talent or skill, gives time to help meet the need without asking for anything in return. In the context of this book, a volunteer is someone who gives time and talent to help extend the mission and ministry of the church.

A decade or two ago, most churches were heavily dependent on women who were not employed outside the home because they were able to give generously of their time and talents to help make the church's program effective. Today more than half of all married women work outside the home and do not have as much time to give to the church as they or their predecessors once gave. Women who do not work outside the home are in the minority. However, these women, in addition to those who work outside the home, remain the primary source of volunteers for most congregations.

Working women are more selective about the kinds of volunteer work they do, and must give fewer hours than they might like to give. Even so, working women provide continuity to church programs because, in most cases, their service is an extension of time they have given over several years. They provide quality to programs because of their experience and training. However, the fewer number of hours they are able to give has necessitated a search for volunteers from other segments of the congregation.

One source of volunteers churches can tap now and in the future is persons who are over fifty-five years of age. These individuals may have taken early retirement or may be seeking additional activity in their lives because their children are grown. These mature adults who are interested in volunteering in the church and elsewhere have skills and experiences that make them prime volunteer material for local churches.

A second source of volunteers is young persons under thirty years of age. Many of these persons are not married or are married with no children. They are skilled and have time available to work in people related jobs. Either type of young adult group can be a reservoir of volunteers for the church so long as the church does not consider them too young or inexperienced.

Although the demographics of who is volunteering are changing, people still are volunteering, and the need for volunteers is as great now as at any previous period. The age, energy level, availability, and degree of experience of the volunteer has changed. Whether or not the church can adjust its concept of the ideal volunteer remains to be seen.

In order to better understand the nature of volunteering today, we will "sit in" on a discussion about volunteering. The six people at the table, plus the convener, will discuss issues related to volunteering.

The six people, composites of hundreds of volunteers, are: John, a retired person who has been active in the church for years; Mary, a forty-year-old married woman with two children who is taking a "birth break" from work; Jim, a self-employed plumber who has a limited church background; Bob, a person in his early fifties who has no church background but who gives time in one of its outreach programs; June, a young, single, working woman in her twenties who grew up in the church; and Elsie, a women in her sixties who has worked in a church for years. These six are a cross section of the core of volunteers in many congregations.

We will drop in on the conversation of these imaginary volunteers from time to time. Their dialogue will keep the discussion down to earth and will illustrate the practical aspects of the principles we are highlighting. In general, their conversation will introduce topics for consideration or summarize points that have been made. Let us listen and learn from them.

The Volunteer Habit

"It's good of you all to have come to this session on volunteering. I know each of you gives time to the church. Let's begin our discussion by asking about your sense of volunteering. A part of this may be motives, a part may be situation, or whatever. Speak out on volunteering in general, if you would, please."

John clasped his hands in front of him on the table. He looked at the other people and nodded. "I'm supposed to tell you about volunteering. Being a volunteer is a normal part of my life. Even before I retired I gave a lot of time to the church." He paused. "There are days when I don't know why I volunteer. I just do it. In a lot of ways, I suppose it has become a habit, a way of life. Being a volunteer, for me, is as natural as waking up in the morning. I want to go to the church on certain days and do something that helps others. As a matter of fact, over the years I've discovered that when someone else is helped, so am I. In the sense that I am personally rewarded because I help another person, volunteering is being selfish. I do it because others benefit, but also because it helps me. When others are helped because of what I do, I feel good."

Mary, on John's right, nodded her head. "I've got some of those feelings, too. Maybe I can't put it exactly as John did, but I don't work, and the church is an outlet for me. It isn't that I don't have anything to do. The baby and the three-year-old are plenty of work. As you all know, I married late. I was thirty-four, and we waited another four years before having Jennie. Now Jeremy is here, and that's it for us. But we decided that I would stay home for six or seven years, until both children were in school, before going back to work. I love my children, but there is another need in my life. I have to have a means of using my talents and my time to help others. The church is one place where I feel my efforts are not wasted and I do help others. In this sense, I see volunteering as selfish. On the other hand, the church has taught me, over the years, that to be a Christian I must let my hands, feet, mind, and emotions work for others. I consider my volunteering through the church a natural outgrowth of the church's training. I also am committed to expressing my

Christian convictions, and the church is the way I do that."

Mary paused and smiled slyly. "I have to add that volunteering gives me a group. My work setting provided this for years, and now the church gives me a chance for social interaction. I need this part of volunteering."

From across the table, June spoke next. "Mary is older than me. Also, she's a mother and I'm not. I'm one of the young singles we've talked about in the church for the last two or three years. I have to deal with the question of volunteering from a personal perspective. I give time to teach in the Sunday school partly because I have heard since I was a little girl that giving time is one way to praise God. My life is built around my commitment to God. That's a key to why I volunteer."

June paused and looked across the table at John. "I'm like John, also. Volunteering is a habit. Tuesday night is set aside for lesson preparation and Sunday morning is teaching time. These are blocked out times in my life. I'm certain that if for some reason I made a change, such as giving up my Sunday school class, there would be two big holes in my life. I teach because I like it, because the kids are great, because I learn much more than they ever will, and because it makes me feel good when the kids do something worthwhile. I also feel that I'm doing what God wants me to do."

The temporary silence was broken by Bob. "Thinking about volunteering in the church is a little hard for me. I don't have a church background. Giving time to the church because it has taught me to do so is not important to me, or to people like me. I wasn't taught that because I didn't go to church. I started going to church a few years ago because of a personal experience with God. But I haven't been going long enough to know much about the church. The part about getting something back because I give of my time is there, though. As I sit here trying to identify what it is I get back, I can't put it into words. The only thing I can say for certain is that volunteering makes me feel good. That's too selfish to admit, but it is a powerful reason to keep on volunteering. I come and work here because I'm good at what I do. I've been trained in a skill, and that skill is needed in the church—the church I attend. Although my job as a counselor is emotionally taxing during the day, the time I spend visiting and working with people in the church is more often than not an uplifting experience. I get more rewards from working in the church three evenings a month for nothing than I receive in a month from my private practice."

Jim, tapping his gnarled fingers on the table, looked around the room. "I give time to the church because it treats me as though I'm worth something. I never figured that people in the church would take me seriously. I haven't got the education Bob has. I'm just a plumber. But a long time ago, a minister came up to my door and asked me to come to church. I couldn't see much reason for going, but this guy came back three or four times. I came to church and told him I didn't think I fit in with the other people. He wouldn't hear of that. He kept after me, and within a couple of years he put me on the trustees. I knew things about buildings and loved it. But, as you know, we can't stay on a committee for more than three years. At the end of the second year he asked me to teach a Bible class. It's hard to admit, but I could hardly read. But he kept after me, and I started a class for a group of my friends—none of whom were in the church at that time. You know us as Jim's Bible

Buddies. It does me a lot of good to share my church with people like myself. Not every church in town will accept people like us because we aren't very educated and we don't like to dress up in suits, but this church welcomes us and gives us things to do. It makes us feel important. Besides, I give time because I feel that God wants me to do something for others because of all the good I've received. I teach because it does me good and it helps others, too."

Elsie, a prim little woman, waited for everyone else to speak before she took her turn. "I've been a widow for nearly thirty years. During those years the church and its people have been my family. Frank, my late husband, and Jim were good friends, and we started coming because of Jim. When Frank died, I had no one else close by except people in the church. It became my home. I gave time and energy because that's what a person is supposed to do in a family—pull their own weight. I know this sounds like I'm pretty selfish about the church, but the church has helped me by teaching me love rather than self-pity. It has broadened my circle of friends beyond the town, and it has shown me others who are in more need than I am or was. The church has helped me to grow and to be a person. That's a good reason for volunteering."

The room was silent for a moment or two before the leader spoke. "Let me try to summarize what volunteering is like based on your descriptions. John said an important part of volunteering is the feeling that he received a lot when he helped someone else. Mary said the church helps her use her talents constructively. She also feels good about helping others and being part of a social group. June feels that volunteering meets her need to obey God's call as well as the church's

21

teachings. Also, her teaching means a great deal to her and to her students. Bob feels that he's using his skills to help people without being paid. That makes him feel good. Jim has said that volunteering includes getting people to church and giving them jobs that make them grow. Besides that, Jim thinks of volunteering as giving something back to God, through the church, for all of the good he has received. Elsie considers volunteering to be a means of being a responsible person in a community. She considers it important that everyone does their share so that the family will continue."

Before we "listen in" on more of this session, it is important to summarize what was said. First, people are still volunteering. According to *Giving and Volunteering in the United States: Findings from a National Survey, 1988 edition*, it is estimated that more than ten million people, much like these six people, gave time through the church. The time they gave, in 1986 dollars, was estimated to be worth approximately $13.1 billion. That's a lot of time and a great deal of money. The testimonies of the people around this table illustrate that volunteers in the church take their commitment seriously and act on their commitment by giving time to help others.

A second important implication of the conversation is that people volunteer because of the personal growth and inner rewards they receive. Volunteering is an ingredient of life that acts much like leaven. Time given through the church is perceived to have more impact on both the giver and the receiver than occurs in other aspects of a volunteer's life. Volunteers appear to feel a commitment to give back to others through the church.

A third implication of the conversation is that the church, because it teaches people the need to give, should provide opportunities for volunteers of all types. Jim was the most outspoken advocate of giving everyone a job in the church, even those who seem least likely to be able to do it well. In Jim's case, he sought a particular group to witness to and minister with inside the church. Without the persistence and guidance of his pastor, Jim would not have become involved in the church.

A fourth implication of the conversation is that people volunteer for a variety of reasons, most of which have some bearing on self-enhancement. According to this group, this personal emphasis is neither wrong nor detrimental to the volunteer or the church.

A fifth implication is that people should be encouraged to use their skills and talents within the church. In this sense, volunteering is an opportunity to utilize existing talents and skills for the good of others through the church.

Volunteers Are Different Today

Although people continue to volunteer, there is a difference between current and previous practice. Let's go back to the group to find out how they perceive these differences.

June began the discussion with a reference to her mother's extensive volunteer work. "I find it very difficult to volunteer for more than one position. Mother used to spend two or three days a week at the church when we were growing up. I know God calls me to work on his behalf, but I don't have the kind of time mother had to give to the church. I'm single and I work. Work cuts out the daytime and some Saturdays and some early evenings. The boss thinks that all single people have loads of time, so we catch the overtime. I'm not complaining, because that means extra money; but, it also leaves limited time for volunteering. Also, I have other interests. My life includes work in the church, but my volunteering isn't dedicated solely to the church. I do some things with other Christian organizations."

Mary chimed in. "I know what June means when she says work time rules your life. I'm not working for now, but I hope to go back in three years. My volunteering will be cut back considerably when that happens. Overtime may not be a problem—except during certain seasons of the year—but the children will be. We have to schedule family time, and that means everything else is cut off. My volunteering will be limited and selective."

Jim spoke next. "As I said, I'm a plumber. That means I'm self-employed. There isn't anyone else to call on to help me make a living. I have to do it all by myself. My schedule gets pretty rough sometimes, and work nearly consumes me. That's the reason I have to limit my volunteering to the Bible class that meets on Sunday morning."

John began to tell about himself. "Work schedules aren't my problem. I'm retired. The problem with me is that I have many interests. I can give time to any one of a dozen organizations in the community and feel good about it. I have focussed on the church and three other organizations. What I have discovered is that I've broadened my horizons. I'm not giving all of my attention or time to the church anymore. At one time, all of my volunteering was in the church."

Bob then added his comments. "I am like John in the sense that my volunteering has broadened quite a bit over the years. I had nothing to do with the church for a good bit of my adult life, and so the volunteering that I did was not in the church. I was looking for a place to use my skills and talents to help others. The church provided that opportunity. If it hadn't, I probably would have gone elsewhere to give time."

Elsie spoke slowly, as though analyzing what she was saying. "Although my life has been centered on the church for years, I am giving more and more time to non-church agencies. I suppose, in spite of my loyalty and commitment to the church, I am giving time to those agencies that can help me make good use of my talents. You may not think a widow like me has a need to be appreciated for skills and talents, but that is wrong. I like to be known for what I can accomplish just as others do."

Finally, the convener attempted to summarize. "I hear what you are saying. Each of you feels a need to give time, but you're more selective now than in the past. Those of you who work seem to be more careful than your parents might have been about giving attention to your own life and being with others such as family. One of the most important things you said, however, was that there is an increased number of opportunities from which you can select to give time to good causes. This reduces the time you can give to the church. You also made it clear that you want to use your skills and talents and will look for the places this can be done best. My impression is that you, as a group of volunteers, are more selective in what you do than previous volunteers."

The last statement of the group convener needs to be emphasized: Volunteers today are more selective in what they do. The church has competition for the time and energy of volunteers. Volunteers choose where to give their time. They do not confine their expression of Christian commitment solely to the church, but choose the place or places where they can grow and express themselves through volunteer activities.

Volunteers Have a Variety of Skills

Volunteers not only have a variety of skills, but they also seek to use their skills in the church. The critical factor in volunteering is whether the church or some other agency will make the best use of these skills. Let's hear what the group has to say about this.

"I'm a plumber, and I thought the church couldn't use my skills," Jim said. "The church doesn't use my work skill—plumbing—except in an emergency. But I have other skills because I run my own business: I have contacts at the bank; I do my own bookkeeping; I am familiar with contracting and subletting; I know the building codes in the community; I am a member of two fraternal organizations; and I am a boss to the people who work for me from time to time. Any one of these skills can be used in the church. In fact, over the years the church has made use of most of them. That's the reason I'm still here rather than in another congregation."

"Jim hit it on the bullseye with me," said Mary. "I worked in a large organization for about ten years before having Jennie. During that time I learned a lot of things, including personnel practices, training techniques, budgeting and planning, supervision, motivating people, and interpersonal relations. This church has encouraged me to use all of these skills, not just the mothering skill."

June nodded her head and added, "Computer

science is my field, and I love it. I have worked with the pastor and layleader to design a system for us, and I have helped to train my church's professional and secretarial staff in the use of particular computer programs. These are skills quite different from the one I use to teach the class on Sunday morning. The church is trying to use the multiple skills I bring from work, education, and life experiences."

People in the church are multi-faceted. They must be in order to live and cope in the current and future social and economic environments. Even when people say that their specialty is "such-and-such," they should be viewed as persons with several skills to give to the church rather than persons having only a work skill. Volunteers are individuals who travel, who are educated, and who hold jobs that demand several types of skills—often including interfaces with computers and strong interpersonal relations skills. The church should not pigeonhole its volunteers, but must encourage them to give a variety of skills to assist in the church's mission and ministry.

Volunteers Want to Get Involved

"You know what really burns me about the church? It gives you Mickey Mouse jobs. I don't want to sit around in meetings all of the time. I'm an active person. Give me something worthwhile to do and I'll do it." Jim hit his fist on the table to emphasize his point.

Mary jumped in. "The one thing that turns me off is working hard on a project and then having no one do anything about it. I was on a committee to review confirmation materials and teaching techniques. We met half a dozen times and gave a substantial report to the board and the pastor. That was three years ago. We haven't heard a word of thanks, nor have we seen any of our recommendations even acknowledged. That, to me, is a terrible waste of a volunteer's time."

June agreed. "Jim and Mary are right. I have enough meetings at work. I'm not interested in sitting through a meeting at night, especially when someone has a bunch of inane ideas to propose. I want to see results, but committees don't get much done."

Elsie was more subdued. "Well, now, the church is made up of a lot of different people, and everybody wants to be heard. June, I appreciate what you say, but the people who propose those ideas don't think they're inane. It takes time to hear everyone and to think through the implications of what they're proposing. I like those meetings. They help sort out what the church is going to be and do."

"You're right, Elsie," June said somewhat contritely. "I was overreacting to the last meeting I attended. I'm glad there are people like you who have the patience to listen and think before the rest of us act. It helps the church move in a positive direction."

Bob spoke up. "I'm kind of a bridge person. I have the same inclination as Jim, Mary, and June, but I know the importance of taking time to listen and plan, much like Elsie. The church is made up of people like us, volunteers. God calls us to be its members. We are its program, its outreach, its mission, and its ministry. Our pastor is here to help train, inspire, generate ideas, and lead; but, without us—the volunteers—not much would happen. I know this, and so do you. When I get impatient, I try to sit back and think about what is being proposed from another point of view. I try to think of questions about procedures, about why we should be doing this or that, and about who should be involved. I try to let God work through me. When I do this, it slows me down and helps me through what could be some tedious meetings."

John added his perspective. "I'm like Elsie, now that I'm retired. I suppose that's partly because I have more time, but it's also because I enjoy the stimulation of some of the discussions. Bob helps to keep us in line during some of our council meetings. I'm not saying that I don't get bored or impatient. I do. I'm saying that I see the need, now more than when I was younger, to let people be heard."

Mary was slow to speak. "Maybe I'll be more mellow when I get older, but I'm more like June and Jim than John. I don't have the time or inclination to sit through meetings. My faith is active. I want to do things. I am not interested in hearing the same arguments every time there is a meeting. I want decisions. I want a course of action to be followed. If there is anything that would turn me off from the church, it would be harnessing me into a job that requires me only to attend meetings. I believe I'd quit."

The church, as Elsie and the others have said, is made up of a variety of people. Each has a need to be heard. Yet, there are some volunteers who are not interested in participating unless there is direct action, such as teaching, working in the office, visiting, or being part of the outreach team in a community. All volunteers are not alike, and most of them want to do something.

A problem facing pastors and other leaders who deal with volunteers is how to separate those who are activity oriented from those who are more inclined to serve on administrative or planning committees. When a volunteer is placed in the wrong job, he or she often quickly becomes uninterested and quits.

Conclusions

These six people have told us a lot about volunteering. First, several have said that much of their motivation for working in the church comes from a personal relationship with God. They feel called to work in the church. This call is the generator for their involvement.

Second, these people have indicated their willingness to give time and energy to the church to help others. They have said that the climate for volunteering has changed for them because of limits on their time. These limits are imposed by work and other opportunities to use their time for themselves, for their families, and for doing good for others. The church is in a competitive mode today in regards to having a major share of volunteers' time. This is quite different from previous years when the church was the primary organization through which one could give time to help others.

Third, these persons have told us that volunteers have a multiplicity of skills. Volunteers want to use more than one skill in the church. They do not want to be categorized, but they do want to be challenged so that they can strengthen skills they have acquired through work, schooling, or life experiences.

Fourth, these volunteers have emphasized the need for the church to be open to using whatever skills people bring to it. The plumber had obvious skills that could be beneficial to the trustees, but his perception was that no other church in the community was interested in using his skills. In time, of course, his other interests became skills that were utilized by the church. The point he made, and which the church needs to hear, is that every person can provide skills as long as the church is willing to accept the person and to find a place where those skills may be used.

Fifth, these volunteers expressed strong opinions about being involved in programs. Some of them wanted to help with the planning and administration of programs, but at least half of them were interested in doing more than planning. These volunteers were not hesitant to suggest that if their skills were not utilized, they would go to other organizations where they could be active.

With this information as the basis for our understanding of volunteering, let us turn now to how we motivate people to become volunteers.

II

Motivating People to Become Volunteers

Volunteers say that they give time and effort to the church because volunteering (1) makes them feel good, (2) is perceived to be both a Christian's responsibility and opportunity, (3) is one way to use one's skills and talents in a helping manner, (4) helps people grow in skills and in grace, (5) is a good way to develop spiritual depth, (6) is a response to the Lord's blessings, and (7) is perceived to be a natural expression of a Christian's life.

Motives for volunteering are not easily isolated. They tend to be combined or mixed rather than a solitary force. The motive of making a person feel good may be intertwined with the motive of developing one's spiritual life. The motive of responding to God's call and blessings may be intertwined with the motive of wanting to use talents and skills through the church. An individual's motives for volunteering in the church tend to be some combination of the seven identified above.

The group's comments in chapter 1 illustrated the interweaving of motives for volunteering. The context in which volunteers function within the church is an important consideration. A person may believe that the need to use talents and skills to help others can be carried out through the church better than any other institution. One variable in the church context that will influence the continuation of this belief is the willingness of the church to find ways to utilize multiple talents and to reward people for giving time.

Duty, as such—a significant motive for volunteering—is not discussed in this book. Instead, this motive is considered to be Christian responsibility and Christian opportunity. These two sides of the same motive are determined by the manner in which church leaders present options for work. Today duty does not have the same motivating force as it did in previous years. This is due partly to an attitude among younger persons that loyalty is not an important commitment when it comes to the church. Many consider one local church to be as good as another when choosing a place to express one's Christian life through volunteering.

Another important motivation for working in the church, which was not mentioned by the group, is agreeing to work as a favor to another person. In one church, four persons volunteered because they were asked by a friend to whom they felt an obligation. Their motive was having a personal obligation to the individual who asked them to volunteer. This motive should not be minimized by church leaders. In fact, this motive may be used to recruit certain persons for key leadership positions.

Volunteering Makes People Feel Good

Jim spoke. "I'm going to have to say again what I said earlier: I feel good when I give time and when people benefit from what I do. That's the reason I helped organize a Bible study class. I don't know that much about the Bible, but I help others learn while I learn. It feels good to be able to be a leader."

Bob responded in this way. "My biggest motivation for giving time for counseling is the feeling I get. Somehow working in the church's program, even though I'm doing exactly what I do every working day, is rewarding. The problems I deal with in the church's program are just as complex and trivial as those I deal with during the day. It must be the context, what I expect of myself, or something. But, I get more rewards here than anywhere else."

Church leaders must remember that people like to feel good about themselves. The desire to be a volunteer in the church is rooted in the knowledge that people who give time feel good about what they do in and through the church.

People who are placed in stressful situations or in jobs in which they do not accomplish what they believe they should are prime candidates for burnout. They quit. It isn't that these people fail, or that others think they have done an unacceptable job. Rather, it is the lack of rewards, either internal—feeling good about themselves—or external—from those who should appreciate their efforts—that is a crucial factor in their decision not to continue as church volunteers. Burnout is more apt to occur because of lack of appreciation than overwork.

This doesn't mean that a church's aim is to have volunteers do tasks so that they feel good. Everyone knows that there are many mundane and repetitious tasks to do in any church. The issue is to vary the assignments so that people have some jobs that make them feel good about the outcomes and themselves. In addition, it is extremely important to give rewards to people for working. People need to be recognized as doing important work for others through the church.

In order to alleviate the feeling of being trapped in a job, it is helpful to put jobs into categories such as administrative, program, maintenance, planning, and so forth. (A discussion of job types is found in chapter 6. The jobs you identify as being able to be filled by volunteers can be categorized.) In this way, leaders can make certain that volunteers are not stuck with the same kind of task for several years.

Volunteering Combines Responsibility With Opportunity

"I have to reemphasize the need I feel to keep up my church membership vows by volunteering," Elsie said with emotion. "Mother used to say we had a duty to help the church once we joined it. Duty isn't the word I use to describe my feelings. I feel that because we are part of a church family, we have a responsibility to carry out our share of the work. We may not accept the responsibility or take it seriously, but it's there nevertheless."

Mary was somewhat hesitant as she spoke. "I suppose my work outside the home changed my perceptions of volunteering. I consider my work in the church as an opportunity. It meets several needs for me right now. It gives me opportunities to practice skills I will need when I go back to work. It allows me to spend time away from small children. It puts me in roles of responsibility in which I have to use my skills and

35

talents. It helps me to meet and work with a variety of people in the church and the community. It gives me a group with whom I can interact on an adult level. For me, volunteering is not a duty or a responsibility. It is a pathway filled with opportunity."

"Your language is a bit romantic for me, Mary," John said. "When you get to my age, you tend to view life a bit differently. I can agree with both Elsie and Mary. The work I do in the church is fulfilling what I consider to be part of the responsibility I assumed when I took membership vows. On the other hand, whenever I volunteer to do something at church, I consider the job an opportunity to meet people, to do good, and to get to know more about myself."

Volunteering is serious business. It is taking seriously one's vows of membership. It is sharing with others to meet the more mundane and necessary tasks of institutional life. It is carrying words of commitment that are often spoken in the church through to action. Volunteering is accepting responsibility and putting feet and hands on the programs of the church.

Yet, volunteering is more than responsibility. It includes searching for opportunities to help others. The help that volunteers give is part of a large circle that feeds back to the original volunteer. Helping others results in being helped.

In a direct way, each task can result in personal growth for the volunteer. Each church job involves developing positive interpersonal relationships with others who may be opposites in temperament and in their outlooks on life. Each responsibility encourages a volunteer to spend personal time planning and to be a manager of energy. Opportunities abound when a person volunteers to work in the church.

Volunteers Use Skills and Talents to Help Others

"One of the best things about volunteering in my church," said June, "is the fact that I can use my training and my talents. I'm involved with training people to use computers at work. The same teaching skills I use at work I can use as I teach a Sunday school class. The information about computers and programs that I have gathered at work have been invaluable in my experience with the church's computer committee. In addition to these skills, I sing in the choir, which is a use of another of my talents. I find that work in the church affirms me as a whole person. Volunteering through the church is my way of praising God. The church uses what I'm trained to do and gives it a spiritual meaning. That's important to me."

"The important thing to me about volunteering in the church is that when I use my skills and talents here, it gives me a chance to help others," Jim said. "At work, I help myself—I am very narrow. I have to be. If I don't focus on my work, people won't use me the next time they need a plumber. So, I use every bit of skill I have to help myself. But at church, that pressure is off. I have a bigger vision. Others benefit by what I do. That's the important part in the use of my skills as a church volunteer."

John smiled and responded, "I'm glad you said that, Jim. Over the years the church has encouraged me to use my skills to help others. This encouragement has meant a great deal to me because it kept stretching me. I had to continually face the question of what purpose I had to serve other than myself. My experience and training had to be worth more to God than I could give back. The church helped me understand that by giving me jobs to do. Those opportunities to do things for others by using my skills have been blessings to me."

Everyone has a skill or talent. Some people need more time to discover the exact nature of their skill or talent than others, but each person can use innate talents and skills acquired by training and experience to benefit others through the church. When the church and its volunteers discover this aspect of volunteering, a happy and active mixture results. People whose skills and talents are used to help others become committed volunteers.

Volunteering Helps People Grow in Skills and in Grace

Jim spoke to the group. "One of the most important things that happened to me was when the pastor asked me to teach a Bible class. I never was one for reading and thinking; I was more action-minded. But, the pastor thought I could grow, and he was right on target. I have grown a lot because he believed enough in me to help me believe in myself."

"Jim, that's the way I feel about working on the church's computer system," June said. "My job at work is pretty routine. Mostly I train people to use the same programs, and once in a while I help someone to complete a report. These are standard procedures. Working in the church isn't standard procedure at all. It helps me to learn and grow. My work with computers in the church is a different type of experience, even though I am still working with computers. But in the church we are experimenting with new ways to use programs and the computer. My work here has increased my expertise at work."

"Volunteering in the church has had a different effect

38

on me," added Elsie. "I was totally turned in on myself before I started to volunteer at church. Over the years I've learned that others face life situations that are as hard or harder than those I face. My work in the church has taught me to be less self-centered and less demanding of others. If this is growth, it is spiritual development—an increase in personal grace. I guess that's the best word. I've grown in grace because I have volunteered in the church."

Volunteers work because they feel they must help make the church a force for good in people's lives. That is the reason volunteering in the church requires not only skills and talents but also grace.

One reason that people grow in grace is they must learn to share. Being forced to accept another person's ideas and attitudes as being as worthy as one's own is a form of growth. Volunteers must learn to share ideas, to sculpt their behaviors to be sensitive to the feelings of others, and to be tolerant of varying degrees of commitment. Working in the church means to grow in grace.

Volunteers continue to work in the church because they see results. June watches the young people she teaches grasp ideas and she sees her commitment to God reflected in them. Jim sees growth in himself and in others. Bob experiences a feeling of accomplishment through his church counseling sessions. Mary's need to do things and to interact with adults concerning important issues has immediate feedback. It is very important for people to see results and to receive feedback. As they work, they should grow, learn, and be rewarded with recognition as well as with the tangible results of their efforts.

Another reason volunteers continue to work is to

improve their skills. Volunteers are able to improve their skills because they must perform more than one job in the church. Each church task requires more than a routine application of a skill to a problem. Growth is demanded because the church deals with the whole of a person, not a skill in an isolated situation. This emphasis on wholeness requires skills of a relational as well as a rational nature.

Volunteers in the church also use their talents. Talents are gifts from God; they are not earned or learned. One is given the possibility of a very good singing voice, a precise memory, a charismatic spirit, and so forth. These are gifts from God that we call talents. A Christian person makes it her or his business to develop these talents in the service of God. Volunteers focus their talents in working through the church.

Volunteering Helps Develop Spiritual Depth

People often have a mistaken idea about volunteering in the church. They believe the church will be the ultimate spiritual place in which to work. They believe the people who participate and work in the church will be paragons of spirituality. They are wrong. The church is made up of sinners. These sinners are seeking to develop their own Christian life patterns. People who participate in a church are helping to forge a Christian life pattern in the context of volunteering. People who volunteer through the church are trying to accomplish two things: (1) to develop the spiritual dynamic of a stronger relation to God in their own lives and (2) to assist others in the church to do the same thing.

The church offers a different type of volunteer situation than is found in most other organizations. The difference is found in the basic emphasis of the organizations. The church's primary emphasis is the development of one's spiritual life. This emphasis is quite different from that of other organizations and agencies. As part of its emphasis on spiritual life, the church teaches the disciplines of spiritual development including prayer, Bible study, and disciplined living. Practice of the disciplines or spiritual development does not automatically rub off on volunteers. However, the context of the church serves as a constant reminder that there is a spiritual way to live.

Volunteering as a Response to Blessings

One of the motives for volunteering that may not be easily understood by church leaders is that of working for the church because of feeling especially blessed. This motive may be perceived as an attempt to assuage guilt. For example, a wealthy person who works as a volunteer in a homeless shelter or as coordinator of a clothing resale shop may be wrongly accused of working to relieve guilt for having so many material goods. This would be imputing a motive. People often work in the church because they feel God has blessed them very much.

The person whose primary motivation is to return blessings to others may seem to be overly pious at times, but piety is to be more commended than condemned. These persons ought to be supported in their volunteer efforts, but they also must be treated as all other volunteers. That is, they must be trained, assigned, and evaluated.

41

Volunteering as a Natural Expression of a Christian Life

The most easily understood motivation for volunteering is that Christians believe they ought to give time through the church as an expression of God's love for them. This is a natural expectation of Christian people. Returning to God a part of one's time and resources is an axiom of a Christian's spiritual journey.

In addition, the kinds of training Christians receive in the church promotes volunteering. Helping others is a theme of the church. Giving to others is a New Testament admonition. Working through the church to assist others is a normal outcome of Christian teaching.

This is not a pure motive, however. All of us are naturally selfish, and as we grow older we are prone to more boldly ask, "What's in it for me?" An answer is that as one practices the Christ-like life, one begins to absorb some of the characteristics of that life. The logic is quite simple. It says anyone who practices Christian living will be giving time, talent, and money to assist others who are in need. Volunteers give time and talent to help others.

June commented, "One of the things I keep telling my Sunday school students is that they need to act in the name of Jesus Christ. I go on to tell them that this can be done best by volunteering to work in the church. This may sound like a pat answer, but it is what I believe."

Even those who have been in the church for a short while understand the need to express God's love through volunteering. This need does not arrive with the blaring of trumpets, but comes with particular force to those who are regular in attendance at worship and in the church school. Giving time for God's work is a natural expression of one's commitment.

Shared Enthusiasm

Although it is not a motive as such, enthusiasm—when shared with members of the congregation—has the force of a motive. People who are challenging in their commitment to Christ can be very persuasive about one's opportunities to serve God through the church. Transferring enthusiasm from one person to another is called shared enthusiasm.

Volunteers can be turned on to working in the church by another's enthusiasm. This turn on may be instigated through the pastor or someone in the congregation who finds attendance and work in the church to be especially fulfilling. This happened to Jim; he was turned on to what he could do and be by the pastor of his church.

Eight Aspects of Volunteering

One of the characteristics of good leaders is that they make church work interesting and fulfilling. Motives may be complex and intertwined, but each motive can be focused by leaders whose intent is to make people feel they are useful to the church and to God. These leaders emphasize eight aspects of volunteering and motivation in their work with individuals who give time to the church. These aspects are the basis underlying a volunteer's bill of rights. (The Volunteer's Bill of Rights, based on these motives, is listed on page 63.)

43

1. Volunteering should be based on interest and commitment. Many church leaders believe lay persons have to be indoctrinated or browbeaten in order to become volunteers. A church that emphasizes volunteer activity bases its presupposition about motivations on interest and commitment.

At times, it may be difficult to understand why an individual wants to work in the church. The person may be unclear about what he or she expects and not be certain about any motivation. It is up to the church to assist volunteers to understand and clarify their motivations. Once this clarification occurs, church leaders can emphasize volunteering as personal commitment to God. Since no motive is pure or simple, it is up to church leaders to assist volunteers to identify their interests so as to express their commitment through the church.

2. Emphasizing work in the church as a personal means of expressing ministry is a second aspect of volunteering. Persons who attend worship and church school know they ought to volunteer to help others through the church. What these potential volunteers need to know as well is that they have a personal ministry. The volunteer knows about collective efforts but seldom does the church discuss volunteering as a means of personal witness and ministry.

The church is a recognizable entity to most people. They know it has a program and a mission. It is important to individuals to know how they can fit into that program and mission while answering God's call in their own lives.

3. Motives may be as pure and as powerful as the wind, but volunteers like to be recognized as contributors to the creation of God's realm on earth. Volunteers like to be recognized for the work they do in the church and also as individuals who are striving to live Christian

44

lives. Church leaders who understand this need can assist volunteers in accepting challenging tasks.

Volunteers need to be treated as useful and important. No church could exist without the work of committed lay persons. Leaders must provide a system of recognition for the work of volunteers.

4. A frequent fear of volunteers is their inadequacy to do a particular job. They may be motivated and willing, but they are frightened. At this point, smart church leaders provide training for volunteers. Training sessions are times to explore the possibility of working in a new capacity in one's life. That was true of Jim and all those like him. He was motivated, but it was the build up of self-confidence that came with positive experience in the church that made him accept a teaching position. Training by whatever method is possible enables volunteers to follow their instincts to work through the church.

It also is important to give feedback to volunteers. Training provides a set of skills. People, as they work, need to know they are doing well or poorly. Accomplishments that are visible must be acknowledged and words of appreciation should be given liberally.

5. Motives to work in the church can be sharpened by a policy telling volunteers that short-term and double-up assignments are acceptable and encouraged. Some people cannot give large blocks of time and yet they want to work in the church. Leaders who recognize time and energy limitations on people can assist people to become volunteers. Motives should not be thwarted by rigid policies of a church that discourages people from giving the time and energies they have available.

Along with this process of encouraging the gift of time is respect for a volunteer's time requests. This is one of the reasons for having a good system for allowing volunteers to exit from their jobs with no feeling of guilt.

6. Another enabling technique for volunteers is limited tenure that is enforced. People may have wonderful intentions, but these are blunted when there is no terminus in sight to their volunteering. There are limits in everyone's lives and these need to be understood by the church. One cannot discuss motives without knowing there are obligations in one's life that preclude giving great amounts of time, or any time, to the church. Other means of expressing one's Christian life must be found, and church leaders are obligated to help people find those other avenues of expressing Christian witness and ministry.

7. A subtle understanding expressed by church leaders is that volunteers like to be treated as insiders. They have a bit more at stake in the life of the congregation than do those who only attend worship and/or church school classes. The investment of time should gain volunteers the privilege of learning more about impending programs and events than persons who do not work in the church's program.

8. Another important right, privilege, or hope of volunteers is the opportunity to get to know the pastor better. This is an important part of being an insider. While it may not be true, volunteers often feel they are closer to the pastor than other members of the congregation. This feeling of being able to approach the pastor easily is critical in motivating some people to become volunteers.

III

Recruiting Volunteers

"How did someone get me involved in the church?" Mary repeated the question she had been asked and then responded, "By asking. It was as simple as that!"

"Come on. It wasn't that simple, and you know it. The person asked you at the right time. You were ready to volunteer or you wouldn't have said yes," John said smiling.

Mary answered, "That's true to an extent, but I didn't know I was ready to volunteer. I had enough other things to do besides giving time to the church. I was pretty much occupied with my family. The big thing about getting me involved was telling me I'd make a difference and asking me to do something worthwhile."

June interjected, "I became involved because I felt it was God's will that I should. People asked me, that's true. They told me I would make a difference, which was important. But most important was my feeling that God wanted me to work in the church. It took a lot of prayer before I made the commitment."

Jim added, "Two things are the keys, at least for me—doing something worthwhile and making a difference. Among my friends, these are the most important factors that can be used to involve them. In my estimation, doing something worthwhile, helping people, and being made to feel worthy of attention are critical to success in recruiting volunteers for the church."

Bob interrupted. "Why else would anyone want to volunteer? I know that's rhetorical, but it questions people who emphasize motives such as duty. I believe people have to feel like they are contributing something to benefit others before they volunteer. At least that's what got me started."

Elsie, more circumspect, said, "Duty does play a part in recruitment. People took vows when they joined the church, and volunteering is one way of fulfilling the vows. As you know, I'm one who believes duty is important. Recruiting people has to include their duty or obligation to the church."

John added his thoughts. "As I think back, I first got involved because a person to whom I owed a favor asked me to do a job. In a sense, I became a volunteer because of the need to fulfill a personal obligation. I agreed to later requests to do other jobs for a mixture of reasons, but the first one was to take care of a personal obligation."

Each volunteer has a story relating to his or her volunteering start in the church. These stories inter-mingle personalities, motives, theology, and life situations. Motives, as we saw in the last chapter, are varied and hard to isolate. Personal traits are difficult to categorize because church recruiters do not give personality tests before asking people to work in the church. Life situations, including a boring or dead end job for which a volunteer is trying to compensate are somewhat more predictable; however, given the number of families with two or more full-time workers, life situations are more difficult to ascertain now than in the past. Combinations of motives, personal interests, theology, and life situations coalesce to make the task of recruiters rather difficult.

A primary issue in recruitment, given the complexity of life, has to do with approach. Regardless of the motives, personal interests, or life situations of individuals, it is the quality of contact that ultimately makes an individual decide whether or not to volunteer. This chapter will examine some of the factors relating to the quality of contact. First we must deal with the issue of who does the recruiting.

Recruiting: A Joint Task of Clergy and Laity

A recurring question concerning recruitment is this: "Whose job is it to recruit volunteers?" Too often the easiest answer is "It's the pastor's job." This is not an appropriate response in many settings. As our discussants verify, recruitment is a joint task of clergy and laity.

Mary summarized the thoughts of some others around the table when she said, "I think lay persons ought to do the recruiting because they know the people; they are aware of the laity's problems related to time, energy, children's schedules, and the like; and they can share the excitement of volunteering in the church with friends."

John nodded in agreement. "I believe it's easier to recruit others such as myself if I or people like me do it rather than the pastor. This isn't true for some jobs, but it is for most of them. I can relate my experience to better advantage than our pastor can."

June added, "Understanding time schedules is important to people like me. I don't believe a pastor really knows the kinds of pressures we lay people are under at work and at home. I'm not blaming the pastor. It's just a different kind of life."

Bob responded cautiously, "I agree that lay people may have more understanding or be more sympathetic to the issues facing volunteers than some pastors, but I don't believe this would be true everywhere. What you are really saying is that a person who wants to recruit volunteers must be sensitive to time pressures, schedules, and the like. I can agree with that; but, from my perspective, the most important thing lay persons can do is to share the excitement of working in the church with one another. When another lay person tells about how working in the church did such and such for him, it means a great deal. In fact, it was the excitement of another counselor that turned me on to work in the church."

Some people respond better to an approach from another lay person than they do to a pastor. Sometimes a lay person may know more about a family or an individual than does a pastor and, therefore, can be more persuasive. In some instances, recruitment is most effective when done by lay persons. Yet, this is not the only approach. Let's listen once again to Jim's experience.

"I've told this story earlier; but, before you get carried away with the importance of lay persons doing all the asking, let me repeat it for you." Jim paused before continuing. "A pastor got me involved. He came to me and asked me to do something I didn't think I was capable of doing. He kept after me, and before long I was a volunteer. He kept pushing me into jobs that helped me to grow and to become a productive member of the church. I doubt anyone else in the church could have gotten me involved."

Bob nodded and added, "The pastor was important to

me, also. The other counselor got me excited, but the pastor provided the solid organizational and missional reasons for becoming involved. I probably would have volunteered without talking to the pastor, but that session gave me a much stronger rationale for involvement."

June agreed. "I talked to the pastor about my feelings of God's call. She understood and prayed with me. Without the pastor's help and prayers, I probably would have heeded God's call, but I would not have been as productive as I have been."

Recruitment by clergy is important, especially when it is done as part of a plan for enhancing the mission and ministry of a congregation and the spiritual and personal development of its members. The plan should be designed so that it prevents a small clique from controlling the church's program and mission, thereby ensuring that church workers are a diverse group and that the people asked to serve can grow into jobs.

The pastor has a unique position that allows her or him to enable the church to be an inclusive and dynamic organization. No one else has this opportunity. However, in order to fulfill these goals, a pastor must have a plan that includes the creation of a large group of volunteers who give time and energy to be in mission and ministry. Part of the plan should be to help volunteers grow in faith and witness.

Recruiting is a joint venture. The pastor's plan may be somewhat different from that of the laity because the perspective of the pastor should be broader and more missional than the perspective of the laity. Lay persons who do recruiting, however, should have a similar agenda in addition to one that is sensitive to the needs of their particular congregation.

51

Tactics for Recruitment

Several methods for recruiting volunteers have proven to be effective. It is interesting to note that these methods are rarely separate. Multiple methods seem to be most effective when trying to recruit volunteers for the church. A brief review of each method can bolster your processes.

1. Visitation by lay persons and clergy

This approach is used quite effectively in many congregations. It is not as simple as it sounds. Several prerequisites are important.

First, a good record system for church members should be kept. The record system should include as much information as is possible about the following for each member: training, education, interests, family situations, and community activities. This is relatively easy to design as a database if the church has a computer system. Although more complex, the record system also can be kept by using index cards. An effective coding process might include a color coding scheme and duplicate cards.

The membership data records are used to select which persons to visit and to recruit for each job. Sometimes the focus of selection will be on an individual's training, sometimes it will be based on education, and sometimes it will be based on an interest of the person. In particular instances, recruitment visits may be based on community activities. The data files are the basis for determining who will be visited and what the nature of the visit will be. A sample membership data form is included as a suggestion.

Sample Membership Data Form

Name: ————————————————————

Address: ——————————————————

————————————————————————

Telephone number: (W) ——————————

(H) ——————————

Family situation: ——————————————

————————————————————————

Education: ———————————————————

Special Training: ——————————————

Current Job: ————————————————

Interests: ———————————————————

Church Activities: ——————————————

Church Jobs: ————————————————

Community Activities: ————————————

Community Jobs: ———————————————

Other: ——————————————————————

Careful selection of prospects from the data files and preparation on the part of the visitation team will result in more effective recruitment. Preparation for the visit should include a review of the job description of the task or tasks the person to be visited will be asked to do and the qualifications of the individual (based on the data record). Also, the recruitment team should discuss the general nature of their approach prior to the visit, including who will be the primary spokesperson. It is useful to have in mind alternate jobs that can be mentioned during the visit if the person refuses the primary job.

2. Using an interest finder

A second method for recruitment is the use of an interest finder. First of all, a distinction needs to be made between a true interest finder and a list of jobs that is circulated to discover who might have an interest in doing each task. An interest finder is a list of possible tasks in the church that tends to run the gamut of jobs. A list of jobs is more limited and changes rather frequently. In the following discussion, the term *interest finder* is used to describe a full list of jobs that may be needed. The term *interest list* is used to describe the more narrow form that is used to recruit people for particular jobs.

A sample interest finder form (partial) is shown below. Note that it does not include all jobs and does not indicate where the jobs will be done.

Sample Interest Finder (partial)

Name: —————————————————————

Address: ———————————————————

Telephone: ————————————————

Best time to be reached: ——————————————

Education: Committee ————— Teacher —————
   AV Coordinator ————— Youth Counselor —————
   Other: ————————————————————

Finance and Stewardship: Committee —————————
   Treasurer ————— Financial Secretary —————
   Financial Campaign Worker —————————————
   Special Gifts Committee —————————————
   Other: ————————————————————

Missions: Committee ————— Spec. Prog. —————
Social Action: Committee ————— Food —————
   Housing ——— Clothing ——— Ecumenical———
   Community Outreach Committee —————————
   Other: ————————————————————

Maintenance: Committee ————— Trustees —————
Administrative: Committee ————— Office —————

An interest finder may be circulated on an annual basis in order to update data files. This can be done by including a form in the weekly newsletter or bulletin for a month. When an update is underway, people need to understand that it is not a call for volunteers, but a request for information.

If the interest finder is used primarily to update member data files, you may exclude some of the items that are identified in the following paragraphs as being necessary to an interest finder. Likewise, if updating data files is your purpose, design the interest finder only to collect data. This will mean that the recruitment teams will have to discuss the other items that are usually included in an interest finder, which is used to recruit volunteers. Do not use the interest finder as a promotional piece to create interest in volunteering.

Several things should be kept in mind regarding both an interest finder and an interest list. First, both must be created on the basis of church needs. Church needs can be categorized as (1) programs, (2) maintenance, and (3) administrative assistance. Programs include teaching in the church school, leading a missions committee, working in social action and outreach programs, singing in the choir, assisting with youth groups, and other types of church programs. In each instance, the emphasis is on designing and implementing an aspect of the church's program. Maintenance needs include serving on the board of trustees, assisting with building cleanup and repair, and serving on the parsonage committee. These are active jobs; however, they can be of an emergency nature as well. Administrative assistance includes working in the church office (typing, mailing, labeling, filing, computer record keeping), acting as financial secretary and/or treasurer, and chairing church committees or groups. The emphasis in these kinds of jobs is on keeping the organization running efficiently. An interest finder or interest list may be divided into these categories in order to help people better understand the church's needs.

The second thing that an interest finder may do and an interest list *must* do is to indicate the basis for volunteering. If a congregation has policies for volunteering, it becomes much easier to recruit and to volunteer. The first policy is to recruit as a means of helping to enrich people's spiritual and personal development. This may seem difficult; nevertheless, personal and spiritual development are the primary purposes of a church. Volunteering is a method for enhancing personal growth (Jim is an example) and spiritual development (June is an example). Two other policies also are important: (1) jobs can be designated as individual or shared, and (2) tasks can be designed to be short or long-term. When these three policies are in place, an interest finder can indicate the basis for volunteering.

Most jobs in the church, including several chairperson positions, can be shared. Any two persons can share jobs, so long as they can and will work together. Sharing allows more people to use their talents for the church. However, careful rules designating authority and follow through should be developed between the individuals who are sharing a position.

Many tasks can be filled by persons with limited amounts of time. Team teaching in church school, so long as one of the persons remains through the year in order to ensure continuity, can accommodate several persons who can devote only a month or two each year to teaching. Ushers, money counters, and liturgists may be short-term jobs, as long as there is a coordinator of these persons. Other jobs require a commitment of a year, such as financial secretary, church treasurer, and trustees. These positions become legal entities and should be filled for the entire year. Even in these positions it is possible to share responsibilities, as long as one person is ultimately accountable and continuity is provided by that individual.

Another policy that may be enacted is to delineate what resources are available to the volunteer. This policy would give specifics about mileage, taxi, or bus reimbursement for doing work at the church or elsewhere. It would discuss how the purchase of supplies is to be done. It also would indicate the kinds of needs each job might place on a volunteer, such as having meal money when taking youth on outings, being expected to pay for dinner when assisting in the preparation and serving of a church dinner, or not being reimbursed for activity sheets purchased for church school classes.

The third thing that an interest list (not an interest finder) should do is specify the place where the work will be done. This is a rather simple listing of the kinds of jobs and their locations (church building, church office, home, church school). The location is quite important for those people who may not be able to come to the church during the day. These people may need to negotiate with church leaders to come during the evening when the church building is open, or to arrange to do the kinds of work that can be done at home.

The interest list should be updated monthly. It will add new jobs and remind people of those jobs still needing to be filled.

An interest finder may include the same kind of items, but it is not job specific and will have a longer list of possibilities for volunteer activities. The interest finder may be circulated quarterly or annually and the data used to update member records.

3. Sign up list

A third means of recruitment is the sign up list. This is a list of jobs for which people are needed. It can be updated weekly or monthly. However, as soon as an individual has signed up for a job, the individual should be contacted and visited. The intent of the contact and the visit is to allow the individual to share with the church recruitment team ideas about the job, and to allow the recruitment team to describe the job's demands. This visit is important because it may result in a change in the individual's decision to volunteer for this particular job.

The sign up list should be put in a visible and easily accessible place. A pencil or pen must be with the list. It usually is best to post one list near the office and another in the vestibule. The rationale for having two copies of a sign up list is that some people come to worship and leave without going to any other part of the building. These individuals can use the sign up list in the vestibule. Other persons come to the church during the week or come into the office area after worship. These persons can use the sign up list by the office or the vestibule. The intent of a sign up list is to make it easier for people to volunteer.

Although some churches may decide to update the sign up list monthly, it is preferable to do so weekly. A change each week indicates to people in the church that others are volunteering. This will be an incentive for those who are considering volunteering to make the move. Recruitment is easier when there is activity than when there is no evidence that others are volunteering.

The sign up list is best used in conjunction with other means of recruitment. Although it may be used alone, many churches view it as a supplement to recruit those who are not contacted in any other way.

Promotional Materials

Recruitment depends largely on promotion or letting people know the church's needs. It is difficult to recruit when members are not aware of the kinds of jobs available. It is equally difficult to recruit when members are regaled for not volunteering. Thus, promotional materials must identify the jobs and indicate how members can grow in their faith as well as expand the mission and ministry of the church by volunteering.

Promotional materials are in part tools for evangelism and in part requests for assistance. Balance of these two components is necessary. In addition to making a request, promotional materials should indicate how each job fits into the total program and outreach of the congregation. No task in the church should be useless, even though several of them are monotonous and lack glamour.

Recruitment materials should be placed in worship bulletins, in weekly or monthly newsletters, and on bulletin boards. The objective is to keep before members the various opportunities for service available through the church. Although church school teachers may desperately be needed, recruitment materials should stress the possibilities for growth and the chances to influence lives through teaching. Desperation does not recruit; opportunities do.

Recruitment materials should specify each job. In this

way the recruitment materials are interest lists or sign up lists. The needs are clearly spelled out in addition to the policies and locations of where the jobs will be done. When one seeks to recruit, one must be specific.

Recruitment materials should indicate which items on the interest list are of a special nature, such as doing preparation work for a stewardship campaign, and which are short-term, such as ushers for a four Sunday evening musical program. These designations will assist potential volunteers to make choices that are appropriate to their time schedules and that coincide with their interests and talents.

Summary

Recruiting volunteers is a continuous effort. It is a joint task of clergy and laity. Several tactics for recruitment that have been effective for many churches include recruitment visits, interest finders, interest lists, and sign up lists. These methods generally are used in combination rather than separately. Be redundant. Give people several chances to hear about opportunities for growth and service.

Promotional materials emphasize opportunities to grow in faith and to have an important influence on others through the church. When the jobs in question are mundane, emphasize the opportunity to work with a group of Christians in a spiritual environment.

IV

Coordinator of Volunteers

"Our church has only about two hundred members and I thought we didn't need a coordinator of volunteers. How could a church with about seventy-five active members afford to have such a person? I swore we didn't need one. But the pastor insisted, and one of our volunteers started working with all of the other volunteers. You wouldn't believe the difference." Mary shook her head in disbelief.

June asked, "What is the difference?"

Mary hesitated before responding. "The most important thing is a feeling of being organized. We get more training and we have a better process for recruiting people. We have about half of our membership involved as volunteers now, as compared to a fourth before the coordinator of volunteers began. One other thing happened, too. The coordinator of volunteers was able to replace some of our misplaced volunteers. They are much happier and are doing a much better job."

June smiled. "We have a coordinator of volunteers, but our church is closer to twelve hundred members. About half of our church is involved as volunteers. We have an extensive outreach ministry that takes a lot of the coordinator's time. She has to make certain the programs are fully staffed every day. That in itself is a job."

A coordinator of volunteers is an important position in congregations hoping to expand their ministry through lay activity. This is the individual who coordinates the increasing corps of persons who want to be a part of the church's frontline ministry. This person links volunteers and leaders into a working unit. The coordinator of volunteers provides the leaven for recruitment and the design for training—two very important needs for volunteers.

A coordinator of volunteers is a key person to those pastors who believe that the church ministers through the mobilization of lay members. The coordinator of volunteers relieves the pastor of administrative and training activities related to volunteers—freeing the pastor to be a pastor.

There must be a close working relationship between the pastor and the coordinator of volunteers because both must be aware of people who can grow and assist in ministry within the congregation. One of the dangers of a poor relationship is that the pastor can negate the coordinator of volunteers by not allowing her or him to actually do the work that is expected of a coordinator of volunteers.

A great deal of mutual trust and respect must exist between a pastor and a coordinator of volunteers in order for them to work effectively and in harmony. The coordinator of volunteers, in order to work well with the pastor, must be aware of her or his strengths and weaknesses. An effective coordinator of volunteers will be in frequent communication with the pastor and with other church leaders. The lines of communication must be kept open, even during times of conflict and tension.

Some of these communications, especially with the pastor, will need to be confidential as they both assess the strengths and weaknesses of volunteers. When the working relationship between the pastor and the coordinator of volunteer becomes irreparable, the one who is the most disruptive of the two should be replaced. It is not always the coordinator of volunteers who needs replacing.

Purposes and Functions of a Coordinator of Volunteers

The discussion of motives and shared enthusiasm in chapter 2 must inform the actions and attitudes of a coordinator of volunteers or a pastor who may need to act in this capacity. It is the leader of volunteers who can best create the atmosphere that encourages and spreads enthusiasm among volunteers.

The foundation for a Volunteers' Bill of Rights is in their motives for giving time to the church. A Bill of Rights for Volunteers will include the following:

1. Volunteers have the right to be recognized and rewarded for their work in the church;
2. Volunteers have the right to assistance in clarifying their motives for volunteering;
3. Volunteers have the right of being assured and of feeling that volunteering is a form of personal ministry;
4. Volunteers have the right to be trained to do their jobs in the church effectively;
5. Volunteers have the right to be assigned to jobs that assist them to grow personally and spiritually;
6. Volunteers have the right to determine the amount of time they can give to the church;

7. Volunteers have the right to be treated as insiders in the church's organizational and institutional functions; and,

8. Volunteers have the right to know and have easy access to the pastor.

This Volunteers' Bill of Rights should guide the thinking and activities of a coordinator of volunteers as he or she fulfills the functions of this job.

The coordinator of volunteers is responsible for six functions that involve several specific tasks. These functions include (1) designing and helping to implement a public reward and recognition system for volunteers, (2) designing and implementing the overall recruitment of volunteers processes, (3) training all volunteers, (4) maintaining and updating lists of volunteers, (5) monitoring the quality of work of volunteers, and (6) evaluating the effectiveness of each volunteer and assisting in the exit and reassignment of volunteers who could do better work in tasks other than the ones they currently hold.

Each function includes a variety of jobs, each of which may take more or less time according to the emphasis of the pastor and the program. For example, the coordinator of volunteers has a function of designing and implementing a training program for volunteers. One of the specific jobs is to select leaders who will do the training.

In one church, the coordinator of volunteers may observe that the pastor is good at training lay persons for administrative jobs. Not only is the pastor good, but she also wants to do most of this type of training. The coordinator of volunteers should encourage this and should design the training sessions to take best advantage of the skills and interests of this pastor.

In another church, the pastor might be most adept at helping with the exit and reassignment processes for volunteers. This difficult task can help relieve the coordinator of volunteers of a function she or he prefers not to do. The pastor's assistance in this job will be an important contribution to the program of this church.

1. The first function of a coordinator of volunteers is to design and give rewards to volunteers. Some people may relegate this function to a lower place on the list; however, rewards and recognition are very important to everyone. Even those volunteers who insist they are not interested and do not need recognition or rewards are encouraged by good words and praise for jobs well done. Everyone needs recognition. The first task of a coordinator of volunteers is to make certain that volunteers receive not only recognition but also some sort of reward for their work in the church.

Recognition does not need to be elaborate, but volunteers deserve to be recognized for their work. This can be done through an annual recognition time for volunteers at worship service or at a church dinner. The intent is for the entire congregation to have an opportunity to publicly thank the volunteers for their time and effort on behalf of the church's mission and ministry.

People like something tangible as a reward. Many churches have found that the use of certificates of merit is an acceptable way of bestowing and accepting thanks. The certificate may be displayed in the person's home or kept among mementoes. It is a reminder to the individual that the church appreciates what he or she has done in Christ's name.

Services of commitment for all of the volunteers are

appropriate in the fall or at the beginning of the year. These acts of commitment usually are part of a worship service and may be held once for all volunteers or at special times during the year for specific groups of volunteers, such as teachers and church school workers on Rally Day or Christian Education Sunday, choir members on Music Appreciation Sunday, mission and outreach workers on Mission Weekend, and so forth. The special emphasis on commitment and recognition is another way to interest additional persons in volunteer opportunities in the church.

2. The second function of a coordinator of volunteers is to design procedures to recruit lay persons to work in the church. It is probable that some sort of recruitment procedures are already in place. Most often, unless there has been a coordinator of volunteers in the past, these procedures will be passed on from person to person and group to group by word of mouth. Recruitment procedures seldom have been written and reviewed and rarely are considered to be policies.

Many churches have no recruitment procedures because no one has put into writing the practices and ideas used to find and enlist volunteers. A coordinator of volunteers makes certain that existing and proposed practices are written and approved by the official governing body of the congregation. In this way the coordinator of volunteers codifies the recruitment process so that energy and time are saved and conflicts over who has responsibility for recruitment in the church are minimized. In this respect, the coordinator of volunteers is the church's "keeper" of the how-to book on recruiting volunteers.

3. The third function of a coordinator of volunteers is to make certain that each volunteer is appropriately

trained for the task he or she assumes. This means that the coordinator of volunteers will design and conduct training for volunteers. Training is the one function that requires the active assistance of the pastor. The pastor must do some of the training or be present at some part of each training session.

Training is a very important ingredient in effective volunteer work, and, therefore, it must be designed carefully. The tenor and effectiveness of training workshops will influence greatly the morale and attitudes of volunteers during the year.

Training includes developing a schedule for training and determining the frequency of the training sessions. Training requires the selection of trainers, most of whom will be laity who have served in the particular positions. It is important to include individuals who are on short-term and long-term assignments in the same training session. The interchange between these trainees will give both groups a better perspective on their roles in the church.

Designing and implementing training is a complex job, even in a relatively small congregation of a hundred members. Individuals' schedules and personal emergencies may make the scheduling of training nights a frustrating if not impossible experience. When a group training schedule is impossible, the coordinator of volunteers should arrange for one-on-one sessions for those who were absent. The coordinator of volunteers also must deal with the hostility of some long-time volunteers who do not feel they need training. It is important to emphasize that everyone needs training at least once every two years.

Identifying the various kinds of training needed (teachers, committee members, administrators, group leaders, and so forth) is a crucial aspect of training. The coordinator of volunteers has a better grasp of the different jobs in the church than anyone else and should be able to group the types of training and trainers to best effect. It is helpful to discuss the typology of jobs and the list of leaders who will be doing the training with the pastor. However, the coordinator of volunteers should be in charge of the training and the trainers.

Materials are an important part of training. Especially important are the materials that contain general rules about driving and insurance, reimbursement of expenses, and the manner in which one goes about purchasing or otherwise securing supplies. The materials specify the needs, opportunities, and responsibilities of each job. These materials should be available to the recruitment teams and should be used in the training workshops. The coordinator of volunteers should write or secure the materials and have them approved by the official governing body of the congregation.

4. The fourth function of a coordinator of volunteers is to maintain up to date lists of volunteers. Lists of volunteers may be created from interest finders circulated at worship or through the newsletter, by word of mouth recommendations from other volunteers or the pastor, and/or from job interest lists that ask potential volunteers to sign up for jobs. Regardless of how the names are accumulated, the coordinator of volunteers must collect them and expand on the information so that the lists (records) can be used for recruitment.

To be most useful, lists must include enough information about each individual for a recruitment team to be able to speak intelligently with the people about jobs in the church. Such lists should include the following data about each person (do not group families—separate them so that each person has her or his own data): name, address, date of birth, educational background, training, occupational experience, current occupation, previous experience in the church, special interests, community work experience, and notes regarding current situations that may encourage or impede volunteer activity. These lists should be updated by the coordinator of volunteers after each recruitment attempt is made by telephone or by personal visit.

5. The fifth function of a coordinator of volunteers is to monitor the quality of work being done by each volunteer. In order to be as objective as possible, this will require a job description for each position. A job description tells the purpose of the position, its general expectations, the specific responsibilities it entails, and who or what group oversees the work. A job description can assist the coordinator of volunteers and others who evaluate the work of volunteers by providing objective criteria for each job. The evaluators may then be more objective in judging the work of each of the church's volunteers.

Creating job descriptions can be a time consuming task, but they are essential to ensure effective volunteer activity and to conduct effective evaluations. The coordinator of volunteers may begin by having each volunteer write the description of his or her job. After collecting these descriptions, the coordinator of volunteers can help the church board establish general criteria for the selection of volunteers for each job. The time given to the creation of job descriptions will be regained during training and evaluation sessions.

6. The sixth function of a coordinator of volunteers is to evaluate the effectiveness of each volunteer. This

means that the coordinator of volunteers has the responsibility of identifying "problem" people and situations and doing something about them. A person or situation that causes discord within the church should be rectified quickly. Usually, the coordinator of volunteers will ask for assistance from the pastor.

Often a problem situation can be dealt with by talking with the people involved and by redirecting their energies into constructive channels. This requires listening and patience, but the benefits to the individuals and the church are worth the effort.

Asking someone to resign or to take another job in the church is difficult and may result in the person's decision to leave the church. Keeping an individual in a job in which he or she is doing only passably well may be injurious to the church. Having to decide whether to ask a person to change jobs or to allow inadequacy to ruin a program is tension filled. A coordinator of volunteers eventually must make this decision, and, with the backing of the pastor, must work with the individual involved. Exit and reassignment processes will be discussed in more detail later.

There may be situations when it is best to help people feel free enough to lay out of the volunteer force for a while. Sometimes a person becomes so wrapped up in a job that the job becomes too personalized. When this happens, it is best to encourage a separation of the person from the job, at least for a short time. This is a delicate task and must be done with much sensitivity. Often this task is performed best by a lay person who may be the coordinator of volunteers or someone chosen by this leader.

Creating and/or enforcing a leader tenure system is one way to prevent church members from interpreting long tenure as meaning that no one else can do the job. It will take a year or two to establish a workable tenure system in churches in which such a system is not currently in place.

Qualifications of a Coordinator of Volunteers

Because of the nature of the coordinator of volunteers' duties, such as individual should have the following characteristics: a pleasant temperament, a people-directed personality, sensitivity, commitment to the church and its program, and the ability to handle tension and conflict constructively.

A coordinator of volunteers should be a pleasant, people-directed individual. It is not necessary for the coordinator of volunteers to be extremely outgoing; however, the individual should not be totally introverted, either. To have a pleasant coordinator of volunteers requires the selection of a person who is not easily frustrated and who is not overly sensitive to criticism from peers.

The coordinator of volunteers must be committed to the church and must be a champion of its program. If the coordinator of volunteers has little or no interest in the church's program, then recruitment, training, and job assignments will be poorly done. The coordinator of volunteers is a key promoter of the church's program.

One of the greatest needs in a church is sensitivity to people's feelings and situations. Too often volunteers are lost to the church because of the insensitivity of a pastor or leader. This occurs because many pastors and church leaders are not able to listen—they are more concerned with talking. A coordinator of volunteers should take time to learn about people and their situations. The coordinator of volunteers must be the one individual in the church who makes it his or her business to be sensitive to others.

The coordinator of volunteers must be able to handle tension and conflict constructively. Every church has its share of tensions and conflicts. If an individual's strongest points are sensitivity to others and the ability to solve conflicts in a constructive fashion, this person should be hired as a coordinator of volunteers. These are the two primary problems that a coordinator of volunteers faces, and the ability to handle them creatively is a desperate need in most churches.

Paid Staff Member? Volunteer? Pastor? Layperson?

A coordinator of volunteers can be a paid staff member or a volunteer who serves as a member of the church's staff. The coordinator of volunteers often is an individual who has served a congregation as a volunteer for several years. Such a person, with training from the pastor (along the lines of this chapter) and the aforementioned qualifications, can be very effective.

It is sometimes better to search for a staff member who is qualified to be a coordinator of volunteers. This staff member can be part of an evangelistic outreach among the membership and in the community on the part of the church. Remember that volunteering should help people to grow personally and spiritually. Efficiency of operation is not as important as having an effective program that assists people in their life journey of faith.

A pastor might want to do this job, especially in a small membership congregation. This might be acceptable except that it is more important for lay persons to handle this job than it is for pastors. If the pastor coordinates the volunteers in a small congregation, the chances are lessened for spiritual and emotional growth among lay persons. Instead of handling this task, pastors could better use their time in visiting, studying, and preparing sermons and Bible study lessons.

Churches that have program coordinators may want these individuals to do the work of the coordinator of volunteers. In exceptional cases, these two jobs may be joined; however, it is best to keep the jobs distinct. The coordinator of volunteers has certain tasks, such as training and recruitment, that can be much assisted by the program coordinator. On the other hand, writing job descriptions, assigning volunteers, keeping track of volunteers' schedules, finding substitutes when some-one is ill or cannot complete an assignment, and evaluating and taking action on these evaluations are time consuming activities that are not usually part of the program coordinator's role.

A volunteer, a pastor (if this proves most desirable), or a program coordinator can function as a coordinator of volunteers in churches with fewer than two hundred persons as the average attendance at worship services. Once above this size, a congregation's activities become too extensive for the pastor or, in general, an unpaid staff member to handle.

In summary, a coordinator of volunteers should be a layperson. The position should be part of the staff of the church. The pastor should support the position and the person serving as coordinator of volunteers. Strong and effective lines of communication should be established and maintained between the pastor, the coordinator of volunteers, other church staff, and lay leaders of the congregation. The size of the church should not affect the position except in determining whether or not the position should be filled with a paid staff member or a volunteer. And finally, the position should not be combined with other positions in the church.

V

Training Volunteers

"How important is training? Well, it's about equal to breathing. You have to do it, but it's so natural that you don't notice it until it stops." John smiled as he continued. "I've been a member of three churches in my life, and I was a volunteer in each one. The first was a large church that had a coordinator of volunteers. She had that place organized! Training was expected, and it was good. The second was a small church of about one hundred and fifty members. I was asked by the pastor to serve on a committee. I expected to be trained. Dumb me. I took the job and was told to use my experience on the job as training; that is, to learn how to do the job by doing it. The third church has about three hundred members, and I belong there now. It has a coordinator of volunteers. It's well organized, too—and training is a big deal."

John continued, "Training happens once a year during September. You must attend two nights sometime during the month. If you miss, you are asked to set a date with the coordinator of volunteers, who will train you herself on a date you can mutually agree on. If you can't schedule a training session, you don't work in the church. It's that simple: no training, no working. The only bad experience I have had as a volunteer was in the church that did not have a training program."

June asked, "Why was that? Was it because the church was small?"

John shook his head and said, "No. The size of the church wasn't important. It was the attitudes of the pastor and the active volunteers that made the situation so poor. As a volunteer, I didn't really know what to do. There was no one to turn to when a problem cropped up, and the people there put great faith in doing things like they had been done for the past fifty years. The situation took away the feeling that I was doing something worthwhile. As a matter of fact, I felt oppressed and used."

Mary responded, "Your description is almost the same as what we—my husband and I—could say about our volunteering experiences. The size of the congregation seems to be immaterial. It is the attitude or feeling within the congregation about the need for training that is critical. Our worst experiences as volunteers were in those situations in which training was not provided."

Jim added, "Without training, our church wouldn't have very many volunteers. Many of our most active workers are people who haven't been involved with the church. They didn't grow up in the church and don't know much about it or what it does. They have to be trained, and they want training. In fact, everybody who is a leader insists on attending the annual training sessions. I know I do."

June spoke again. "One of the things I've noticed in our church is an increase in the number of Roman Catholics who are becoming Protestants. In each of my training classes three years ago, and then again this year, I met half a dozen former Roman Catholics. I was amazed at what they didn't know. But, they come from an entirely different system than ours. They don't understand how important lay people are. It was a good thing they received training."

Elsie cleared her throat before she spoke. "When I first started working in the church, I was put with people who had been working at their church jobs for several years. It was expected that I would learn the ropes, so to speak, from them. That was all right, but several times I felt that these people weren't doing things by the best method, or that they were fudging a little because they were tired. Several years later we got a minister who had these new fangled ideas about training and tenure. It took him more than three years to get the changes through the board, but training became required and tenure—in our church it was three years—was enforced. I had to lay out for a couple of years and then had to go through training sessions before I could become a volunteer again. What a difference it made in my ability to function as a church worker! After the training, I knew where my job fit into the scheme of things. I knew about being reimbursed, about who to call when something went wrong, and I even had a job description. It was the first time in all my years that I had fun."

Training volunteers for work in the church is a necessity, not a luxury. We live in an increasingly complex world. Trustees must continually be updated on the new codes being imposed by several levels of government. Church treasurers must be aware of various and changing requirements from the IRS, the state treasury, and local taxing bodies. Each of these agencies requires some type of report. Insurance coverages are very complex. Volunteers with this type of expertise must help interpret the details of various coverages. Training is needed because of these and a multitude of other types of rules and regulations imposed by agencies of the government.

In addition to bringing certain persons up to date with governmental requirements, training has other benefits. Training makes it necessary for church leaders to work out job descriptions, to identify the skills needed for each job, and to look for people who can effectively do the jobs.

These things sound good, but how does a church go about changing attitudes about training? When does training actually begin? Attitudes change when the training program becomes a reality. As for when training begins, it begins at the time of recruitment.

Training Begins with Recruitment

John said to the group, "When does training begin? When you ask a person to do a job."

Another group member responded, "How do you mean? That's recruitment."

"True. But recruitment—if it is to be effective—includes basic training experiences. Let me explain." John adjusted his collar before he continued. "Suppose you're the one being asked to do a job and I'm the one doing the recruiting. We have gone through the preliminaries about your interest form and the church data base which includes your employment, education, and other characteristics. Now it's time for me to get down to basics. I have to describe the opportunities for service available in the church for a person with your interests, background, and skills. What do I have to tell you?"

Without pausing, John continued, "That's a rhetorical question, of course. As a recruiter, I have to tell each person three things. By the way, these things will be repeated during the training sessions. I have to tell this person the nature of the job and its responsibilities. This will not be as detailed now as it will be at the training session, but it will place the job in the total context of the ministry of the church. At recruitment, a person will know the importance of the job they are being asked to do.

"The second thing I must tell the person is the expectations the church has about the job. This will include a brief description of the fact that a person working on behalf of the church is really its ambassador or representative. Because of this, the church expects the individual to personify the teachings of the church to as great a degree as is possible.

"The third thing I need to tell the person is how much time will be required on a weekly, monthly, or annual basis, and what the schedules are currently for the meetings that the person being recruited will need to attend."

Mary applauded. "That's great, John! If we did all of that when we recruited people, then we might be more successful. People wouldn't be caught unaware about meetings or time commitments."

John smiled and said, "I appreciate your support, Mary. There is one more thing we have to do at recruitment. We have to leave some printed materials with the prospective volunteer. These materials contain two types of information. One section will be on the general procedures of the church, such as who's in charge, when the office is open, the names of people to ask for specific types of help, phone numbers to use in emergencies, and policies regarding reimbursement, use of equipment, and purchase and use of supplies. Another section will be on expectations of volunteers, including doing their jobs well, meeting deadlines, working with others, expressing commitment through their jobs, and being aware that they represent the church."

In this description of what needs to be included in the recruitment phase for volunteers, John has described a preliminary training process. Each of the items mentioned should be included in the first training session for all volunteers. This kind of repetition is not detrimental but reinforces the training procedures.

The second training session should be specific to the job. These two sessions may need to be repeated for those who are not able to attend one set of sessions. In fact, it might be a good idea to schedule both sessions (one and two) during weekday evenings and to repeat them on consecutive Saturday mornings.

Volunteers may take one of two kinds of jobs—short-term or long-term. Long-term jobs usually are committee leadership responsibilities, whereas short-term jobs run the gamut from task forces to committee work. A major difference is what can be done during one's tenure. Training, especially the second session that focuses on the specific needs of a job, differs somewhat for these two types of jobs.

Training for Long-Term Jobs

A rule of thumb is to ask volunteers to take a job with no more than a year's commitment. This allows a congregation to utilize the talents and skills of a relatively large number of persons in a three-year period, and it gives volunteers a termination date. Some jobs, such as trustees, chairpersons of certain committees, and lead teachers in the Sunday school, need persons to lead or be members for more than one year. This need relates to the requirement for more continuity in mission and ministry than might be possible with an annual change of leadership.

A training session for volunteers with long-term jobs is divided into two phases: a general orientation and a session detailing the requirements of specific jobs.

1. General orientation

A general orientation training session consists of four segments. The first segment is very important. It is a description of the total program of the church and a discussion of how each job makes the program work well. This segment is done first in order to help people better understand the second segment.

The second segment is a discussion of the purpose of the church and its goals, and of how the program is the means for meeting the church's goals. Do not short-change either of these segments by mistakenly believing that everyone knows these things. They do not. Even if they do, it will be helpful to repeat the information.

The third segment of the general orientation is a careful review of the literature that was given to volunteers when they were recruited. Be certain to discuss both types of information in the literature—the general operating procedures of the church and the expectations the church has of its volunteers. It is important that everyone understand the material in the literature and the policies it contains. It is equally important to answer all questions relating to the policies and expectations placed on volunteers.

The fourth segment of the general orientation is to discuss what volunteers can expect of the church—especially its leaders—in terms of assistance, resources, guidance, and supplies. It would be useful to talk a bit about the Bill of Rights of Volunteers (see page 63) and how these rights will be met during the time these persons are working. All of this information should be written and given to the trainees as part of the orientation. In fact, distributing this information can be used to lead into the second part of the training, which usually is done at a different time.

The orientation session may be conducted in an hour and a half or less. The session must be thorough, and the people who attend must have everything that is discussed during the session in written form. A brochure or a small ring binder are good methods for ensuring that the information presented at the general orientation session is taken home for future reference.

2. *Specific demands of the job*

The second phase of training is conducted in smaller groups. Each group is specific to the job being undertaken by a volunteer. For instance, all of the members of a mission committee would receive orientation at the same time, whereas Sunday school teachers would be trained together at a different place and possibly at a different time. The second session of the training is job specific and is not generalized to all groups of volunteers.

In small membership churches, it is advantageous to train all program committee members at the same time, and to train teachers at a separate session.

The first objective of the second training session is to bring the newcomers on board by sharing the plans and the history of the group with which they will be working. Each group should have a three to five-year plan in its area of responsibility, which means that it is important for new people to understand the past accomplishments and the future hopes of the group. This is an important aspect of the training session.

The discussion of current responsibilities and future plans leads into a discussion of requirements regarding the attendance of each volunteer at group meetings. A schedule of regular meetings for the year should be shared, as well as any predictable times of heavy work. For instance, the stewardship committee would meet more often as a group, as well as in sub-groups, during an "Every Member Canvass" emphasis than it would at other times of the year. Everyone on each committee or group should be aware of the schedules and crunch times. Each member should feel that he or she is so important that the committee would have difficulty meeting its responsibilities without his or her presence at every meeting.

The schedule of meetings should not be excessive for program committees. Much of the work for missions, for example, can be accomplished by individuals or subcommittees. This would make monthly meetings of the full committee unnecessary for most program groups.

It is during the second training session that a discussion of assignments is held. Although no assignments are given at this time, each member of each group should be apprised of the probability that he or she will be asked to do specific tasks. These tasks will vary over the year, but all of the tasks will be within the job description under which the person volunteered.

The next part of this training session deals with materials and supplies. Volunteers learn how to order, purchase, store, use, and share materials and supplies pertaining to their jobs. It is vital that everyone understands that he or she must be conservative and responsible to the congregation for everything they use in working for the church.

Every job in the church has deadlines that must be met. Volunteers need to know what these deadlines are and how to plan their work in order to meet the deadlines. In this session it is wise to illustrate how to plan backward from the deadline in order to allow enough time to complete a task.

An illustration of "calendaring" may be useful. A committee must have a report completed for the board on May 1. The committee begins planning *back* from this date so that they can meet the deadline.

The report, in preliminary form, will need to be ready for committee member reactions by March 15. The committee will review the preliminary report, and a subcommittee will rewrite it by April 15. The committee will meet between April 15 and April 30 to finalize the report and to decide who will present the report to the board.

In order to have a preliminary report by March 15, the committee must do its research and must have the component parts of the report completed by February 1. This means that the subcommittees responsible for each component will need to do their work in

November and December and to write their reports in January. The resulting calendar looks like this:

October—Committee organizes tasks and creates sub-committees.
November and December—Subcommittees collect and analyze data.
January—Subcomittees write reports.
February 1—Component reports ready to share with the full committee.
February 15–March 1—Committee meets to bring component parts together.
March 15—Writing subcommittee has preliminary report ready for full committee.
March 16–April 1—Committee meets, revises report, writing subcommittee rewrites report.
April 15—Revised report is ready for committee review.
April 15–30—Committee meets to approve report and assign a report group.
May 1—Report is presented to the board.

It may be helpful to use this scheme as a part of the training session. Planning begins with the date of accounting and then a calendar is built backwards.

The final part of the second training session includes a discussion of any special working conditions pertaining to specific jobs. For example, volunteers in a soup kitchen would need to be alerted as to their specific place of work in the kitchen or serving area and as to how rotation takes place so that one person has several jobs over time. Special working conditions relate to the following: the place where volunteering will occur, any unusual situations (such as a class of physically disabled youth who will be coming to the church for worship and Sunday school every second Sunday of the month), and the kind of equipment being used. These discussions will provide every volunteer with identical information so that they will be able to assist one another in doing a better job in ministry.

Training for Short-term Jobs

Persons who have jobs with tenure of a year or less receive the same training as persons with a longer assignment. The general orientation session should be exactly like the one outlined for long-term volunteers. The major differences below relate to the place of the jobs in the program of the church. The second training session should include at least the following seven items.

1. The first priority is to describe what is to be accomplished by each job. Because most of the short-term jobs are program related as opposed to administrative or maintenance related, this description is critical. These volunteers need answers to questions such as the following: Where do ushers go to get the bulletins? What time should ushers be at their posts? What dress is expected? Are there any special requirements? When do the money counters pick up the collection? How is the counting done? May one of the counters use a check to buy all of the coins in the collection? What happens to the money after it is collected?

These are the kinds of information people who are short-term volunteers need. Be specific. Be practical. When short-term volunteers do not do their jobs well, the church's mission and ministry suffers. No one else picks up the programs they may drop or do poorly.

2. A second item is to identify those who will be working together on a committee or in an activity. It is at this point that some people may need to be asked to take a sabbatical or to change their committee or job assignments. During this session, some persons will discover they have difficulty working with certain individuals. It may be necessary to create a specific job for a talented person who wants to volunteer but who feels that the group to which she or he is assigned is not stimulating or action oriented. Take the opportunity to shift assignments following this training session.

3. The third item is a discussion of where the resources and supplies are and how to get them. This is a very practical aspect of the training. It should not be omitted nor given short shrift. Volunteers need to know these things if they are to function well.

4. The fourth item is scheduling and calendaring. This part of the session should include a discussion of deadlines or special dates that require specific preparation, such as an Easter presentation by the elementary classes of the Sunday school. Special plans or dates for practices should be shared at this session, although no assignments should be given. The total needs for getting the group prepared and exactly what is involved should be discussed.

5. The next two items can be handled by giving everyone a preprinted card. One side tells the volunteer who to call for help related to his or her job. This may be the chairperson, the pastor, or someone else in the church. A telephone number is required.

6. The other side of the card tells who has the key to the building in case it ever is necessary to get into the building when it is locked.

7. The final item in this training session identifies, for each volunteer job, whom to tell when a job assignment is completed. This is an important part of training because it relates the job to the entire congregation's

expectations. It is especially important that volunteers have someone to report to about specific tasks because it gives the volunteer a sign off. Some types of jobs requiring a report of completion include painting a room, driving a vehicle on a trip, counting money, or being a chaperone for a youth party.

Annual Training for All Leaders

It is important to have annual training sessions for all leaders for two reasons: (1) the goals and programs of a church change somewhat each year, and (2) new persons are added to the volunteer corps each year as others drop out because of tenure rules, moving away, or other matters that prevent them from volunteering for another year.

A church in mission and ministry should have a new set of goals with a somewhat revised emphasis each year. This does not mean that the church must change all of its program annually. The church should evaluate and change emphases as needed, however. For example, a church with the goal of forming an evangelism committee one year may have a goal of reaching fifty new families with the message of Christ through their church the next year. The goal for both years may be church growth, but the goal is approached quite differently one year as opposed to the next.

An effective three-year tenure rule means that a third of the volunteers in any given year are new recruits. Thus, a church has a new group of beginners every year. These persons need training, but they also need to be mixed in with experienced volunteers quickly. This is done more easily at the annual training sessions than in any other manner.

Training Newsletter for Leaders

A quarterly or semiannual newsletter designed to help volunteers do their work better and improve their skills can be very beneficial. Such a newsletter should include any new policies under discussion regarding volunteering or workers in the church. The newsletter might indicate changes in insurance that could affect volunteer activity in the church, as well as tell of special seminars or workshops offered by conference or ecumenical bodies or high schools that would be helpful to volunteers.

Some congregations use the volunteer newsletter to applaud the work of specific volunteers or groups. The newsletter need not be long, and can be published irregularly during the year.

VI

Giving Assignments

The group members looked at one another and then at John, who was shaking his head. Mary asked, "What's the matter, John? Did you have a bad experience with an assignment?"

John frowned. "I wouldn't call it bad, but I did have a rather difficult experience with an assignment once. It only happened that one time, but it has influenced my thinking ever since." He paused. "Do you want to hear about it?"

June, speaking for the group, said, "Of course we do."

"Well, I guess it was partly my fault, but . . ." He looked around the group and smiled. "We got a new pastor in our church who, I thought, was gung-ho about using volunteers. It was exciting to listen to him talk about how lay people are the church—how Christians are the embodiment of Christ and act in his name. That kind of talk takes hold of a person. At least, it got to me. I volunteered. I wanted to be a part of this work.

"I asked to be on the mission committee, and the pastor did me one better—I was made the chairperson. It kind of overwhelmed me, but I was determined to do the best possible job for the church. We didn't get any training, and I didn't know a thing about the job. But, as I discovered later, neither did the pastor know anything about helping a person to be a good chair of the missions committee. Not knowing anything didn't stop the pastor. Not a bit."

John paused and then continued, "He came to our first meeting and he took over. I had the mistaken belief that as chairperson I was responsible for opening the meeting, setting the agenda, giving out assignments, and closing the meeting. Silly me. The pastor did all of those things. Maybe it was because I was a little slow and somewhat self-conscious. I was a lot younger then. But I don't think it would have made any difference if I had been twenty years older and a lot faster on the pick-up. This pastor wasn't going to let lay people be in charge of any program in his church.

"I didn't know that at the first meeting, however. It was after the third meeting when I was talking to some of the other lay people who had been appointed to be chairpersons that I learned the sorry truth. Every one of them had the same story to tell as me. The pastor had given us each the same kind of assignment and then had nullified our work by taking over for us."

Jim asked, "What did you do? I would have quit. I don't have time for those kinds of shenanigans."

"I'm afraid I was too green and hopeful to resign. I stuck with it for a year, but by the third month it was a struggle to do anything. I couldn't have cared less about the church or its mission program. In fact, we didn't have a mission program, or much of anything else. A pastor just can't do everything in a church. Unfortunately, the pastor we had then never really learned that. He went from church to church talking about lay

91

involvement and then excluding lay persons by not letting them be in charge of programs."

John's experience is more common than one would like to believe. It takes courage on the part of pastors to allow the church to be an expression of lay persons. Those pastors who train laity in basic Bible study, teach and demonstrate ethics, encourage innovations, and trust God to guide the church are in places where vital Christianity is being lived. Those pastors who believe that they are the only persons who can guide the church are in churches with frustrated lay persons and membership and attendance declines.

Why Use Volunteers?

Jim spoke to the group. "One of the lessons a pastor taught me a long time ago was that we lay persons have a great deal to contribute to others. I still can't believe this pastor asked me to be part of the leadership of our church. In my eyes I had nothing to contribute, and yet he called me." Jim shook his head in disbelief.

June interjected, "As I was growing up in the church I often heard how important I was. I didn't believe it, but the pastor and other leaders asked me to be on this group and that group. Before long, I felt like I had something to offer." June smiled and added, "That's a super feeling."

Lay persons are the eyes, ears, feet, hands, and hearts of a congregation. They are not professional religious people whose thoughts are on the institution. Lay persons' lives may include many personal activities of piety, but they live in a very competitive, cynical, and topsy-turvy world most days of the week. They know what it means to live out one's commitment and beliefs in an indifferent and sometimes hostile environment toward religious expressions. Efforts of lay persons to live their Christian beliefs are hard work and seems to have few visible rewards. Because of their experiences in trying to be Christian in the world, it would be strategically smart for lay persons to do much of the work of the church.

On the other hand, lay persons know some of the buttons to push that could get others to attend functions and activities of the church. They know of people who might be interested in participating if such and such time or activity were adjusted slightly. When motivated and trained in spiritual disciplines, lay persons—individuals who live in the world—can be the church, indeed. They, more effectively than pastors, can communicate the Gospel through actions to persons like themselves.

Lay people can extend the influence of the church because there are so many of them as compared to the number of clergy. One pastor can relate well to fewer than fifty members of a congregation. Groups of lay persons expand those numbers geometrically as they reach out to other lay persons. If lay persons are empowered to be evangelists, then the possibilities of outreach can be overwhelming.

Every Job Is Important

John continued the discussion. "If you ask me, every job in the church is important. I've done maintenance jobs like cleaning the sanctuary and setting up chairs, I've worked on committees, and I've taught in the Sunday school. I felt that every one of those jobs added something to me, and that I contributed to the life and ministry of the church where I was."

June nodded. "I don't have near the experience you've had, John, but I've done my share of jobs as I've grown up in the church. And I felt good about every one of them. They all counted for something."

There are no unimportant jobs in the church. After all, the church is a vehicle through which the ministry of Christ is performed. People who work for Christ through the church are important in the sight of God. No one should belittle any of the people or the tasks they undertake. Assigning jobs should be accompanied by an expression of appreciation for each individual's contribution to the church's life and outreach.

Each job is different. Volunteers need to keep in mind that some jobs are more public than others, which often makes these jobs seem to be more important. Being assigned to a nonpublic job, such as cleaning or being Communion Steward, is as important as being a Sunday school teacher or choir member. Even though some people are more visible than others because of their jobs, each job is important in the total ministry of the church. Chairpersons of committees are seldom identified as "public people," but their behind the scenes work is critical to the church's program. Both types of jobs are necessary and equally important.

Another difference among jobs in the church is that some are performance oriented. An organist, choir member, lay speaker, usher, and similar jobs have demands related to public performance. Not only are those jobs public or visible, but they also require specific training and skills. Not everyone can play the organ or sing well. These skills are acquired through training and can be used to glorify God. These skills should not, however, lead one to diminish the skills and gifts of others on which the church depends to heal, counsel, clean, and publicize.

Neglecting to assign certain types of jobs, whether they be unpleasant or mundane, will hurt the church in the long run. Such neglect can hurt the church in two ways. The first is that jobs needing to be performed—duplicating, mailing, cleaning, filing, maintaining a member database, or whatever—are left undone. However, hiring people to do jobs because the jobs are "dirty" or boring is not a good practice. This is the second way that neglect can hurt the church. For every job pushed aside or "hired out" because it is unimportant or unnecessary, some volunteer is lost to the church. Jobs are windows of opportunity for lay persons. When a window of opportunity is closed, the volunteer cannot perform a service of ministry or mission. Volunteers should be assigned to all types of jobs in the church.

Types of Jobs

The church can offer volunteers a wide selection of jobs that can be grouped into five categories. Job assignments should be based on an individual's interests, talents, and skills. Every effort should be made to assign an individual to a job that is a best fit for her or him.

1. The first category of church jobs involves the physical appearance of buildings and grounds. This sometimes is called maintenance activity or trustees work. These jobs are designed to keep the buildings,

church, and parsonage or manse in good condition and the grounds of these buildings looking attractive and neat. In some small congregations in rural areas, the grounds are kept by a nearby resident who mows the grass and keeps the church yard cleaned of debris. In other places, volunteers assist paid janitors by doing some of the cleaning and minor repairs. Sometimes, volunteers are asked for assistance only on those occasions when work must be completed quickly and when the tasks are simple, such as painting, scrubbing floors, or getting church school rooms ready for occupancy.

2. A second category of church jobs involves activities around the office that demand varying degrees of skill, such as typing, duplicating, and filing. In many congregations, office jobs require schedules that permit volunteers to go to the church building when the office is open. Some churches have a policy that enables some of these activities to be done at home by persons with the appropriate equipment. A volunteer can do a great deal of typing at home, either on a typewriter or word processor. In either instance, the completed work then can be taken to the office where it can be duplicated. Having the flexibility to allow work to be done off premises has enabled many churches to utilize volunteers who otherwise could not give time.

3. A third category of church jobs includes those that make personal contacts such as visiting, delivering tapes as part of a tape ministry, being a youth group counselor, or teaching in the church school. These activities make the volunteer an obvious representative of the church. Therefore, volunteers assigned to these jobs need to be chosen and trained carefully. Such jobs might have a service period of a few months to ensure that a wide variety of persons represents the church in its public contacts. Even so, volunteers for these jobs must be made aware that their attitudes and demeanor

have much to do with the effective mission and ministry of the church.

4. Another category of high visibility includes performance tasks such as singing in or leading a choir, being a worship leader, or ushering. The volunteers who fill these jobs must be selected on the basis of talents and abilities, and must have some general training. It is possible that some training can be done by the church or leader (choir director); however, in certain performance jobs this becomes difficult. In the process of selecting volunteers to serve on performance teams, church leaders need to choose those who can grow into the jobs and to work with those who already are adept at the jobs.

5. The fifth category of church jobs is committee work. In fact, the major amount of work in churches is done by committees. These groups of volunteers are in charge of the programs of the church and actually make these programs function. Committee members perform unsung activity as they select curriculum, take care of finances, educate members about missions, and help plan worship services that meet the needs of the parishioners. Committee members should be interested and trained in specific aspects of a church's program. They are indispensable even in those churches in which pastors try to do the entire program by themselves.

It is very important to match the interests, talents, and skills of volunteers with the types of jobs best suited to them. Even when the primary aim of an assignment is to help a volunteer grow, the assignment must not seem to be overwhelming. Assignments must be judged—by the volunteers and by the person making the assignments—to be compatible to the needs and interests of the volunteers. Do not attempt to assign a job to a volunteer whose life patterns and personality are incompatible with the job.

The person making the assignments must be sensitive to volunteers' perceived weaknesses when giving assignments. If a volunteer is assigned to a finance committee but has absolutely no interest in money, a mismatch has occurred. A mismatch eventually causes a volunteer to drop out and perhaps even to become inactive in a church. Skills and interests must be matched with job types when making any assignment.

Long- and Short-Term Assignments

The difference between long- and short-term assignments was noted in chapter 5. This distinction is very important, if not in the eyes of church leaders, at least in the minds of volunteers. Assigning persons to jobs on either a long- or short-term basis must be done according to the preferences and time schedules of volunteers.

1. Short-term Assignments

Jim smiled at the people around the table and said, "I don't have one problem in getting Harold, Billie, or even Jerry to do something for me. They never come to church per se, but they help me out any time I call. The reason they are willing is that I only ask them to do something that can be done quickly and that involves physical effort." (Jim didn't say it but he knows the skills, talents, and interests of his friends. This is a point to keep in mind by those who give assignments—know your people.)

Elsie chimed in, "That's the way I get my friends involved, too, Jim. They aren't willing to tie themselves into jobs that will not be completed for a long time. They want to help, but on terms that fit their lifestyles."

The life patterns of many persons suggest that offering opportunities to volunteer for short-term assignments can allow those persons to express their ministry and still have time for other things. The combination of church work and free time is very important to the volunteer. The need for both may seem to be a cop-out to some purists, but volunteers live most of their lives outside the scope of the church.

Working for the church is only one of the many ways Christians express ministry. Church leaders should understand that volunteers can be in ministry with their families, at play, at work, as well as when doing a job for the church. The church does not and should not have exclusive rights to the total free time of any volunteer. One of the church's tasks is to help volunteers do jobs that fit both their life patterns and their time commitments. In many cases this means offering many short-term options for volunteer work.

A short-term assignment is something that can be done quickly—in a few hours or in a month. Some congregations make it a policy to use several people on a short-term basis to type bulletins, paint, trim shrubs, clean gutters, and check in supplies. This policy spreads the work, allows several people to help the church, and gives volunteers access to jobs that meet their time schedules.

A primary emphasis of short-term assignments is to utilize people when they can work and to design jobs to fit the availability of volunteers. Congregations who make this emphasis in their policy have discovered that more people volunteer than church leaders could have imagined.

2. Long-term Assignments

The primary emphasis in long-term assignments is the development of and continuity in church programming. For example, it is difficult to have a strong church school if there are new teachers every month or two. On the other hand, a lead teacher with a three-year assignment can train and use several people as aides who can then work with her or him on short-term assignments. Using persons who have long-term assignments to help train others is an important role that can be incorporated into long-term assignments.

Long-term assignments allow the church to give people opportunities to add new dimensions to their lives. Jim, one of the discussants, added several new dimensions to his life through long-term assignments in the church. He grew in ministry because of the trust that he felt church leaders had in his abilities.

For some people, long-term assignments come only after a series of short-term assignments. This shift occurs because someone among the church's leaders— a Coordinator of Volunteers, for example—encourages people to become involved in leading the development of the church's program.

A problem with long-term assignments is that they sometimes appear to have no end. Although some church leaders may not like the idea of a tenure system, such a system is quite important. A supportive tenure system requires one year off after three years of service, and asks that leaders use the year off to be engaged in spiritual development through Bible study. The year off may be spent taking an evening course or two at the local adult school to better prepare the individual for some future assignment.

Long-term and short-term assignments are equally important. Both kinds of jobs can be used to help people express their ministry. Churches should have at least twice as many short-term as long-term assignments available for volunteers. When this is the case, training schedules must be adjusted to care for the larger number of volunteers at the short-term training sessions.

Making Assignments

Eight things must be remembered when making assignments.

1. Be specific, give clear directions, and don't assume that the volunteer has any knowledge of the job. Elsie reminded us of the value of training when she described how she, for the first time in her long time career of working in the church, became clear about what she was to do. After her training, Elsie began to enjoy working in the church. Her training involved careful and specific explanations of how to do the job to which she was assigned.

2. Tell what the job involves in time and energy. This is especially important to persons whose schedules are jammed with inflexible job-related demands. People need to know how often they are expected to attend meetings, for example.

3. Tell each volunteer the kinds of tasks that must be done, and, if applicable, mention the need for public appearances. One volunteer was quite willing to work hard on any assignment as long as she did not have to

101

be in front of a large group. This was discovered after an embarrassing confrontation between her and the committee chairperson who expected each person to make a short presentation to the congregation about the committee's activities.

4. When making an assignment, make certain to have available any materials the volunteer will need in order to do the job. If this is not possible, include the securing of supplies as the first phase of the job. Supplies might include paper, typewriter ribbons, stencils, paint, ladders and brushes. A volunteer who comes to work is ready to begin, and it is up to the church to be ready for the volunteer.

It is important that any equipment to be used by the volunteer should be in good working condition, unless repairing the equipment is the job of the volunteer. This can be accomplished through good maintenance. Of course, equipment can break at precisely the wrong time. Volunteers understand this and will help to repair the equipment, if possible. However, sloppy maintenance and obvious disregard for equipment tells the volunteer that a good job is not necessary.

One duty of every job is to keep a supply inventory. This can be accomplished by giving a simple form to the volunteer weekly or monthly or at the start or end of a job.

5. Set a time to begin and a time to end each job. Volunteers need to know both ends of the allotted time for their work activity. In some cases, it is sufficient to give a range of time for a job. For example, a volunteer asked to do a mailing may be told that it usually takes between two and three hours to complete the job. This allows the person some leeway in getting the job done and gives the individual a yardstick against which to evaluate her or his work.

It is helpful to monitor the time it takes for different volunteers to do various kinds of jobs. Collecting these data allows a coordinator of volunteers to do a better job when assigning tasks to various volunteers.

6. When volunteers are working, have someone available for assistance by phone or in person—in case unforeseen problems occur. If a volunteer is typing at home, she or he needs to know whom to call if a question about format arises or if he or she runs out of materials. It is equally important for a janitor or a trustee to be present when volunteers are painting so that additional supplies can be secured and so that strict safety standards are observed.

7. The person who makes assignments should evaluate the quality of work done by every volunteer on every job. This is usually an impossible task. A system of verbal or written reports in addition to some observation on an irregular basis is usually the best monitoring procedure that can be established. Evaluation must be more frequent and more intentional for those jobs whose results are evident to members, constituents, and the general public. Mailings, publications, making and displaying signs, and performance or personal contact are examples of volunteer jobs needing to be monitored carefully and regularly.

8. The person who makes assignments should note any problems encountered by volunteers on any job. It is equally important to become aware of jobs that have special needs, such as extra insurance, security precautions, or bonds for people who handle finances.

At best, giving assignments is an awesome responsibility. It can be very rewarding if the assigner follows these eight suggestions and treats the volunteer with much respect. Without the volunteer, either the job will not be done or the assigner will have to do it.

VII

Evaluation, Rewards, Resignation

"If you ask me, persons who work in the church don't need to be evaluated. That's especially true if they have been trained for their job." Elsie was more emotional than she had been during any of the three previous sessions. "I think that if the trainers have done their job and the assignment has been done carefully, then all the evaluation that needs to be done has been done."

"You have a couple of good 'if's' in there, Elsie," Bob said, trying to be supportive. "What if the trainers didn't do a good job and the assignment didn't fit? What if the person wasn't paying attention when the most important parts of the training were being presented? What if the volunteer thought that he or she knew more than anyone else about doing the job? What if the trainers allowed a person to skip a session? Evaluation is one way of making certain that everyone knows what is supposed to be done, and that they are proceeding in the proper direction."

Jim responded, "I don't like to be evaluated. It kind of rankles me—especially at the church. I was opposed to it when the pastor talked about it because we're all working for nothing to begin with. Then he helped me to understand how important it could be. Every time I do a plumbing job, I am evaluated. People either like the way I do it, or they don't invite me back. That's pretty harsh, but business works that way. When you think about it, evaluation at church makes sense. Why should we let people mess up the church's program? They should be evaluated on the job just like me."

June nodded and said, "I don't like to be evaluated, either. I feel as though the Lord wanted me to teach a Sunday school class. Besides, those kids are quick to let me know when I'm boring or don't make sense. But, we have a new boss at work who is into evaluation. She wants us to be the best that we can be. She set up a system that evaluates us so that we can improve and so that we can see what our strengths are. I can tune into those reasons for evaluation. In fact, I've come to appreciate what evaluation can do for me."

Evaluation

Evaluation is the act of comparing what is done with what is supposed to be accomplished. It is a time when deeds are measured against goals. In most instances, people consider evaluation to be a trying time, no matter when or where it is done. However, if evaluation is done correctly, it can be a means of support, training, and redirection. The evaluation process and end results are key factors. Using a few principles of evaluation in the church helps people to grow and the total program to become more effective.

The individual in charge of giving assignments must make each volunteer aware that evaluation will occur. It is helpful to write the approximate date (month) when evaluation will occur on the assignment sheet so that the volunteer will know when to expect it. A discussion of evaluation, including the format of the process to be used, should also be part of the training. If these measures are taken, volunteers will not be surprised by the act of evaluation.

Although a standardized evaluation format will not be appropriate for every job, use one for as many jobs as possible. Standardization helps to relieve the feeling among volunteers that someone is "out to get me." The four major parts of a standard evaluation format are goals, schedule, resources, and the identity of the evaluator.

1. When giving an assignment, help the volunteer to list one or two goals that he or she should accomplish through the job. One of the goals may be personal and one may be related specifically to the job itself. These goals must be reachable and measurable. It will take some time to negotiate these goals. Both the volunteer and the person giving the assignment should agree to the goals. Record the goals on the assignment sheet.

2. Each volunteer should have a time schedule so he or she knows when to expect evaluation. Evaluations, except in unusual situations, should occur after the volunteer has spent several months on the job so that the individual can become acquainted with the duties and opportunities of the job. This time span will give volunteers time to decide whether or not their goals are within reach. If, after this time, the goals are deemed to be too easy or impossible to reach, new goals should be set.

3. The person giving the assignment must tell the volunteer about the resources needed for the job and how they are to be made available. This list of resources should be detailed so that during evaluation an

individual cannot claim inadequate resources or lack of information about resources as a reason for doing less than an effective job.

4. When an assignment is made, the identity of the person who will be evaluating the volunteer should be given. The name of this individual must be stated and put in writing so that there is no mistake about who will have authority over the job in which the volunteer will be working. The named individual should conduct the evaluation interview or secure someone else to do it.

These four guidelines can alleviate potential disagreements and surprises at evaluation time. Following the guidelines will force persons who are giving assignments and conducting evaluations to standardize their approaches. Growth should occur for both the volunteers and the evaluators.

Evaluation is effective when it is fair. This means that church leaders should recognize unusual situations. Such situations must be the exception. Evaluation, in general, should employ a standardized process.

Scheduling times for evaluations is quite important. In most churches, evaluations can be conducted in June after much of the Spring programming has peaked. The first step of evaluation can be a self-evaluation checklist of accomplishments and perceived problems. The self-evaluation form should include a place to write the goals agreed on at the beginning of the year. The checklist should evaluate the training and the support for the volunteers, and the effectiveness of the job done by each volunteer.

Self-evaluation forms should be sent to the volunteers two to three weeks before they are to be collected. After the self-evaluation forms are collected and analyzed by the appropriate persons, personal interviews are then scheduled. A brief letter should be sent to the volunteer that gives information about the time and place the personal interview will be conducted. The letter should tell the volunteer who will be conducting the interview and who is to be in charge of the total evaluation process. The letter also should state that the volunteer may request that another church leader be present in the personal interview, or that someone else do the interview.

Evaluations are to be shared with the person being evaluated. This provides an opportunity for exchange and growth on the part of the volunteer and the evaluator. This sharing session may be conducted a week or two after the evaluation interview. Part of the evaluation sharing session should include the recommendation of future job assignments and the selection of one or two personal goals. The job recommendations and goals should indicate to the volunteer that she or he is a valued member of the church's volunteer corps. In summary, the evaluation should demonstrate to the volunteer that the church is trying to utilize her or his skills and talents in both a personal and church ministry.

Rewards

"I like to be recognized. I tell myself I don't need recognition, but it makes me feel good to know that someone thinks my work is useful," John said smiling.

Elsie interjected, "It may surprise all of you, but I have all of the certificates and mementoes that the church has given to me over the years that I have worked in it. Our church gives certificates every year, and I keep them. I don't know that they have any value to anyone else, but I can look at each one and remember what I did that year. The certificates are a living memory for me."

June continued the discussion. "When I first volunteered, I knew that I was doing what God wanted me to do. It felt good. Then, at the end of the year, our church had a recognition service for all of us teachers. The Sunday School Superintendent gave each of us a certificate and a little cross. This one," June pointed to a small cross in her lapel, "is the first one that I got. It means a lot to me—more than the other certificates and things I've received since that first service. I like the recognition services, the certificates, and the little gifts. These things are visible reminders of my commitment to God."

Everyone likes to be recognized. Unfortunately, the task of saying "thank you" to volunteers is neglected by many churches. Somehow, in not recognizing the work, effort, and commitment of volunteers, churches express a callous belief that lay volunteers owe something to the church, and that there is no reciprocal debt. This may be true. Vows taken when one becomes a member are binding. However, the church owes volunteers and members something as well. The church, especially the pastor and elected leaders, owes each volunteer a thank you. When the church makes no effort to express thanks, it becomes increasingly difficult to recruit volunteers. People feel that they do not want to work in a place where no one ever recognizes their efforts.

If churches will follow five simple steps regarding commitment and rewards, the morale of volunteers will improve immensely.

1. Plan an annual commitment service for volunteers who are beginning their jobs. This service can be included as a part of the worship service. The service should not be long, but it must let volunteers know that their work is important to the church. Many hymnals and books of worship have brief commitment services included in them. If this is not the case, special services can be secured from denominational headquarters or religious bookstores.

2. At the conclusion of each school year, many churches have a service of recognition for the work volunteers have done. This service of recognition can be done during the worship service. Although such a service usually is conducted during June, it can be done any time. This service might require half or more of the congregation to go to the front of the worship area to be recognized.

At the times of recognition and commitment, the worship bulletin should include a special section that lists the name and job of every volunteer. Creating this list is time consuming, but adds greatly to the recognition and commitment services. The bulletin also becomes a "certificate" for the volunteers to keep.

3. Give each volunteer a physical token of appreciation. This token can be a certificate, pin, Bible, or cross. It is surprising how many volunteers put these things away and then, one day, bring them out to walk through the life of pleasant memories they have had in working for the church. Without giving physical tokens, a church robs its volunteers of opportunities to show others a part of their lives.

4. Every once in a while a church should give a special award for an outstanding volunteer's work. This award can be given to an individual when he or she retires from a lifetime of work in the church, to a leader of the building committee when a building program is

completed, or to a key volunteer when a mission project produces a major church endeavor in the community or the world. The special award may be a distinctive certificate or a book of some sort. The important thing is that the award recognizes an important deed done for the church by a volunteer who has given a great deal of time and effort. This special award is not like an award that may be given to people who make large monetary contributions to the church.

5. "If you see your name in print, be sure that it is spelled correctly." These words should challenge every pastor and coordinator of volunteers. Two things are important about this statement. First, it assumes that people *will* see their names in print, and, second, it admonishes those who are responsible for the names to be certain of the spellings.

Whenever possible and appropriate, a church should print the names of people who are working on projects or serving on committees in bulletins, newsletters, and news releases. The idea is to let everyone know that work is being done by lay persons—with names. Listing names has an attractive power, both in the church and in the community. Others may be motivated to become involved in the church because a friend or acquaintance has been noted as working as a volunteer. Listing the names of people who work in the church is an important and necessary part of good stewardship of volunteer personnel.

Resignation

"There are two kinds of resignation in our church," Jim said. "One is when you do it yourself; the other is when you are asked to resign."

Mary responded with surprise: "You mean that volunteers are asked to resign? That's great! I wish that was a policy in our church."

"It's a policy in our church, too, as far as I can tell," June chimed in. "I know two of my friends were asked to take different jobs because they couldn't do the ones they had signed up to do. My friends were a little put out at the time, but they loved what they ended up doing."

"That's not resignation; that's transfer. They were put into other jobs." Mary said.

"The option was to take the other job or to lay out for the year. In my eyes, that's resignation," June replied.

A multitude of intrusions occurs in a person's life during a year. Such intrusions may be illness, the loss of a job, a job change, family changes, or family increases such as a birth or a child returning home. Any one of these changes may be disruptive enough to cause a person to resign from his or her volunteer position.

Church leaders should accept a volunteer's resignation without casting a stigma on the individual. Regardless of how situations appear to an outside observer, life's situations often seem to be beyond one's control to the person involved. Putting an individual through "the third degree" is not within the rights of church leaders. Volunteers should have the right to quit for reasons they feel are serious enough to demand their resignations.

It is probable that some volunteers will not be able to do their jobs well because of lack of training or personality conflicts with the people with whom they are working. In these cases a transfer or a resignation may be in order. This decision should be made by the pastor and the coordinator of volunteers. Once a decision has been made, do not hesitate to make changes. Refusing to make a decision or to implement a decision that has been made only makes an unpleasant situation worse.

When the problem is inadequate training, it may be possible to correct the situation by assigning a mentor to work with the volunteer. This can work if the mentor and the volunteer establish a good working relationship that is mutually beneficial. The person who assigns the mentor to the volunteer should monitor the situation carefully. The mentor should have a short time—perhaps four to six weeks—in which to effect the assistance he or she has been assigned to do.

When a volunteer resigns because he or she has been in a position for the extent of time allowed by tenure, the individual should be recognized for a job well done. This kind of resignation should catch approximately one third of all volunteers each year. These volunteers should be recognized for their work and should be encouraged to use their year off as a time of learning and recharging.

Reassignment

A most difficult task related to resignation is the task of asking the individual to take a new assignment. When reassignment is deemed necessary or appropriate, this difficult task may be made less difficult by following a few simple rules.

1. The best time to reassign an individual is during training. During training, reassignment is relatively easy when it becomes apparent that an individual is inappropriate for the job to which she or he has been

assigned. Although conversations between the trainer and the volunteer can simplify the process, it is possible that the volunteer may refuse the new assignment. If that is the case, you may want to use the procedure outlined in rule 7.

2. Let the first three months that the volunteer is on the job be a probationary period. Assure the volunteer that no stigma will be attached if he or she quits or is asked to change jobs. When this is a clearly stated and known policy, volunteers will not consider requests for reassignment as personal attacks. After the policy has been in effect for two or three years, it will be expected that some people will be asked to change assignments during the three month probationary period.

3. Schedule two or three personal conversations with volunteers, make specific suggestions as to how the volunteer can improve—before proposing any change in the volunteer's job. It is helpful, and imperative in some cases, to have a written record of these conversations and to send a follow-up memo to the volunteer that includes the suggestions made for improvement. Most of the time, these written records are merely precautionary, but they can prove to be useful in some cases.

4. When asking someone to accept a reassignment, offer the individual a job with equal status as well as the option not to take a job this year.

5. Problems do not go away; they must be solved. Therefore, do not hesitate to act. This is particularly true when disgruntled people are involved.

6. When asking an individual to take a new assignment or to resign, find ways within the church to help the individual express his or her personal ministry. This will require considerable effort on the part of church leaders; nevertheless, helping people to express their ministry is part of the job of church leaders. Sometimes giving an individual a special assignment

under the guidance of the pastor or other church leader may be an effective way to handle such a situation. In other cases, asking volunteers to work with a church-related agency in the community may be best.

7. If, after personal conversations and suggestions for improvements, an individual refuses to change jobs, and if you believe a change is needed . . .

    a. make the change. Because this will cause some negative reactions, the pastor must be willing to support the decision.

    b. replace the individual with another person. It is helpful not to appoint someone whom the displaced volunteer considers to be a personal enemy.

    c. work at restoring the damaged relationship. Do not allow a disagreement over an assignment to cause a person to leave the church. Take the initiative to visit the individual and to bring him or her back into the church in a mutually agreeable way.

It is never pleasant to be told that you are not doing well; however, sometimes this message is necessary. One of the axioms of life is that one can do some things well and some things not at all. This is as true in the church as elsewhere. Someone in the church must make volunteers aware of this truth in order to assist them in investing their energies in the most productive ways. Ministry is important and requires our best energies. No one should be encouraged to waste time or energy in inappropriate ways—especially in the church.

VIII

Special Situations in Volunteering

In some churches certain situations can be considered special. These situations may be due to church size, a particular configuration of members, or other factors that make it necessary to extemporize when dealing with volunteers. The intent of this chapter is to anticipate some of these situations and to provide pointers that will enable church leaders to handle such situations creatively.

"One of the things I have learned is that small membership churches have a different attitude toward volunteers than medium sized churches do," John said as he looked around the table. "The biggest asset and the greatest liability of small membership churches is their size. They are small enough for people to know one another well, but they aren't large enough to do much programming."

Elsie nodded and said, "The programming bit is really true, but the worst thing that happened in our little church was that the people who were called leaders were power hungry and didn't let others have a say in what the church was going to do. They had the money and they told us what was going to happen."

Mary responded, "That doesn't happen only in small

membership churches. One of the churches we attended had almost fifteen hundred members, but it was influenced—almost controlled—by one family. They gave a lot of money and expected to be listened to. It was not a good scene."

"One of the things that I've noticed," said June, "is that churches sometimes don't adjust programs to fit the people in the church or the community. A church must adjust its programs to let everyone have a part in the ministry. Each church has a different group who must be made to feel that the church is the vehicle through which they can answer God's call in their lives."

These comments illuminate the situations most commonly faced by church leaders in special circumstances. A review of how other congregations have dealt with these situations can be useful to your church.

Small Membership Churches

Three problems affect small membership churches in regard to volunteers. First, the limited number of people who are available to volunteer may not allow the church to have a strong tenure rule. Second, a small group may control the church and may decide not to include new people in leadership positions. And third, the meagerness of the program limits variety which, in turn, dampens people's interest in working in the church. Although these problems may seem to be insurmountable to some pastors and lay leaders of small membership congregations, these problems should be viewed as challenges. Let's think about these three problems in terms of two possible solutions.

"One of the major difficulties in the small membership church I attended," John said, "was that the pastor didn't let us do much work. Maybe that was our fault, but he brought it on himself. He seemed not to want us to do much more than show up on Sunday morning and be at board meetings to approve what he was doing."

Several people around the table nodded in agreement.

"That was true in our church until we had one pastor who we thought was pretty lazy," Elsie chuckled. "He was lazy like a fox. He was the one who made us take training courses. Can you imagine being trained to teach a class of three kids? He did it. He told us that we expected teachers in the local schools to be trained, and that we should be trained, too. That's the way he began. It was logical. So, we did a few things differently and, before long, we discovered that lay people were in ministry. We were the church, and the pastor preached, visited, and trained. We had an active congregation until he left. The next pastor thought we were acting too much like ministers. It didn't take us long to fall back into letting him do the work."

As Elsie points out, one of the solutions to limitations in a church's size is to empower lay persons to help design and carry out the church's program. Not every congregation needs to have the same kind of program. People who live and work in a given area know what can be done and what may be needed. These church members can become program experts if a pastor can give planning, spiritual direction, and training. Lay persons also can help to design a process that includes recruiting and training new volunteers. Lay persons should be about God's work in their world. Helping them do this is the church's role.

Sometimes it takes a considerable amount of patience and stimulation to help lay persons work out a program and become interested enough in the program to suggest that others might want to be part of the volunteer corps. A part of the difficulty often is a historical unwillingness on the part of pastors to empower lay *persons* to be lay *leaders*. The pastor who takes the time to cultivate and train volunteers will have a church that has an effective program—regardless of the church's size.

Another solution is to revise the program—even the program suggested by lay persons—to make better use of the interests of potential volunteers. A church program is only partially for its members. The primary purpose of the church is to spread the Gospel. This means that a church's program should be designed to attract those people who do not come to church. This does not mean that the program should neglect current members and attenders. However, to think that the program of a church is only for that church is to miss the point of the Gospel of Jesus Christ.

Small membership churches can train, support, enable, and empower lay volunteers. Simply because a church has a small nucleus does not mean that the church cannot be creative. Enabling volunteers to express their ministry should be a key component of any program in a small membership church. With this as a key, the pastor's roles should be to preach, train, teach, and visit.

Large Membership Churches

Having many members on the church membership roll does not mean that a congregation is enabling its lay persons to be in ministry. It is just as difficult to find volunteers for leadership in large membership churches as it is in small membership churches. The difference is the scale of the programs.

Large membership churches that are doing a good job of involving people as volunteers follow four principles.

1. They do not hire clergy to do most of the work. If they hire people to do some of the work, they tend to hire lay persons. Some of the most effective large membership churches depend almost entirely on lay volunteers. In congregations that depend on volunteers, the ministry of the laity is noted and spoken about inside the church and in the community. Such churches have discovered that persons who are willing to give time to work for the church carry into their tasks a zeal and commitment not often found among those who are paid to do the same jobs.

2. Churches that empower volunteers stress the need for lay persons to provide leadership for the church. In most of these churches, potential church members are asked to commit to becoming volunteers during their initial discussions with the pastor about joining the church. There certainly is nothing wishy washy about the request of these churches for lay persons to become involved in ministry.

Large membership churches that utilize lay persons to a great degree are very careful in designing their training programs for volunteers. These churches believe that those who have been taught how to do their jobs are much better volunteers than those who rely on previous ventures in volunteering. In such churches, nothing is left to chance regarding the training and recruitment of volunteers.

3. Effective large membership churches do not rely on a single recruitment strategy. They have discovered the fallacy of relying on a single method of getting

people involved. Their recruitment processes are systematic (many use a database computer program to keep up to date with member interests, schooling, and skills) and thorough (no one is neglected—everyone is asked to do a specific job).

4. Large membership churches with a large corps of volunteers keep their clergy staffs to a minimum. Some of these churches have two pastors, a senior pastor and a visiting pastor or an associate pastor, who are each in charge of one aspect of ministry. Other large congregations have a senior pastor and a lay administrative assistant. The most effective large membership churches rely on lay persons to be in ministry rather than hiring additional clergy.

High Percentage of Elderly

One of the population groups who have many skills and talents and who have energy to give through the church are persons who are sixty years or older. Some of these persons are retired, although many between sixty and seventy years of age hold full-time or part-time jobs. In many cases, retired persons continue to work either to earn extra money or to stay fit.

Generally speaking, age seventy-five and younger tend to be active, persons between the ages of seventy-five and eighty are more sedentary, and most persons over age eighty are hesitant to engage in much activity—especially if the activity takes them away from their places of residence. Thus, it is important to determine which age group is to be the focus of attention when recruiting for volunteers. The following discussion relates to persons who are between the ages of sixty and seventy-five.

A congregation with many members age sixty and

121

older needs to be intentional in using these persons as volunteers. This can be done in three ways.

First, the congregation can establish networks of active elderly people who can serve as leaders in developing and maintaining a care ministry. A care ministry is a good way to provide daily interaction between older church members. Participants in the networks make calls—once in the morning, once in the afternoon, and once in the evening—to older and disabled persons who are unable or unwilling to go out. In addition to making calls, the networks can do shopping, provide transportation, and include certain elderly persons in hot lunch programs (delivered to their homes). This type of ministry is set up by volunteers and, in many congregations, is supported as an outreach activity of the women's group.

Older persons have many skills, much experience, and are willing to use their skills and experience as volunteers in the church. Churches can utilize the talents of older persons for programs of outreach in the community such as tutoring, teaching English as a second language, organizing and administering food banks, or providing skill training for other volunteers or unemployed persons. In churches that use them, older volunteers often become the most dependable group of volunteers.

Churches with a large number of older volunteers have discovered that money must be budgeted for the transportation of these volunteers. Sometimes the transportation is provided by a van purchased by the church and a driver who is a part-time paid or volunteer staff member. The van is used to bring persons to the church for meetings and worship. The van or other form of transportation may be used, on certain days, to drive the elderly on shopping trips or other errands.

When volunteers use their own cars to transport persons for the church, it is imperative to offer the volunteers reimbursement for the costs of providing the transportation. This expense should be considered part of the normal program budget of a congregation.

High Percentage of Two-Worker Families

Two-worker families are very interested in activities that can help them improve themselves and their families. They also like to influence the direction and type of activities in which they and their families participate. While it may seem an imposition of extra demands from the church to ask them to volunteer, this group of people—when they have opportunities to be leaders, planners, and doers—are quite likely to volunteer. They represent a substantial portion of the current population.

The increase in the number of two-worker families over the past decade has changed the shape of the work force and the life patterns of millions of people. Churches with large percentages of these types of families may use four tactics to enable more of these types of members to be in ministry.

First, churches with many two-worker families should allow volunteer work to be done in homes. This work includes holding meetings in the home and doing office and administrative tasks, such as updating a membership database, in the home. Quality controls and specific deadlines are important when work is done in the home. Such controls might be not allowing any confidential information to leave the church and, if a computer is involved, having at least one backup disk of the same information stored at the church.

A second tactic that can be used to involve two-worker families is to schedule church work, such as meetings or work days, so that it coincides with the free time of those wanting to volunteer. This may result in more weekend activities and fewer night meetings and activities. When held, a night meeting should not last more than one and a half hours. Meetings should begin on time, should be run so that all of the necessary business is cared for, and should end on time. When there is a great amount of slippage in meeting times and the duration of meetings, members of two-worker families either will not come or will leave the meetings early. Such individuals have other obligations that claim much of their attention.

A third tactic that can be used to involve more volunteers from two-worker families is to emphasize short-term jobs. A church must have volunteers who take long-term jobs and who act as the anchors in the church's volunteer corps. When there is a solid core of long-term volunteers, many other projects and programs can be divided into short-term jobs requiring one to three months of service. These short-term jobs can be viewed as apprenticeships, as training, or as a means of widening the opportunities for volunteers to become active.

A fourth tactic for involving two-worker families is to encourage the development of two-person leadership teams that may function as chairs of committees. The team can be a husband and wife or it can be an arrangement that links an experienced individual and an inexperienced individual. The objective of having team leaders is to provide leadership in vital program areas of the church while allowing persons with limited amounts of time to function as volunteers. Both persons in a team must receive the same amount of training. Careful attention must be given to defining the kinds and amounts of authority of each person in the leadership team.

These four tactics have been used successfully in congregations with a large number of two-worker families. Churches must continue to find ways of enabling people with limited amounts of time to be in ministry.

High Percentage of Single Adults

Adults who are unmarried represent an increasing segment of the population. These individuals can become a significant volunteer resource for those congregations who are willing and able to attract them.

Churches located near apartment complexes, town houses, and condominiums may have a high percentage of single adults. Often, these singles are of various ages. A successful congregation will adjust to the phenomenon of a large number of single adults and will take advantage of this vital group by recruiting them and training them to be volunteers.

One way to encourage single adults to volunteer and to perform ministry is to start a single adult fellowship. The fellowship group can serve as a focus for adult singles. However, the process for organizing such a fellowship is not as simple as some church leaders would imagine. It takes nearly a year of background preparation, planning, and contacting before the first meeting of such a fellowship can be held. It then requires constant work to recruit and train leaders and to plan programs to maintain the fellowship. Single adult ministry is a specialty; however, when practiced well, it can have significant rewards for the church and for the participants.

A characteristic of single adults is that they will be more transient than other types of volunteers. Single adults have much to do with their time, but they spend their time willingly with those groups that capture their interest. Because their interests change often, single adults have limited loyalty to a church. Thus, it is important to maintain frequent communication with and between single adults. Because of the transiency of single adults, it is wise to train several single adults for the same job. In one year it may be necessary to substitute leaders in certain jobs several times because singles leave the area, change jobs, or have other significant life transitions.

Churches with a large number of single adults tend to rely on short-term assignments for these volunteers. Single adults have more of a tendency than other types of volunteers to take several weekend vacations during the year and to become deeply involved in work at various periods. When short-term assignments are the norm, more single adults can be involved.

Since single adults are more transient and can work more easily in short-term settings, it is helpful to have single adults work in small groups rather than alone. This gives them others to whom they can relate and eliminates the need for constant job training. Group members will be learning together, and the chance for all of them leaving at once is significantly less than for one to leave.

Single adults, no matter the age or reason for singleness, need to express their ministry through the church. Congregations that try to create ministries specifically for this group, that plan volunteer activities around their transitory nature, and that rely on small groups of single adults are more likely to have a good core of single adult volunteers.

Small Clique Running the Church

Sometimes small groups tend to control the church and its programs. This often occurs because of the importance of a family group, because of the historical alignment of decision makers, or because other members of the church have decided not to express their ministry through the church. Allowing a small clique to control a church is tantamount to letting the church kill its members' desires to express their ministry and mission through the church. Only when all members of a church can be in ministry is the church a viable and vital organization.

Pastors who find themselves in such situations must be careful but insistent when making changes. The following six suggestions will be hard to implement, but they can be done with a minimum of ill will and loss of face for those involved. Do not attack incumbent leaders; help them to follow and endorse these steps.

1. Enlist incumbent leaders to design and implement planning for the new program. Help them to reach out into the future. Show them possibilities, but do not threaten them unduly. (Any planning is a threat to those in power.)

2. Insist on involving new people in leadership. This may be difficult, but it can be done over a period of two or three years. Do not introduce a new slate of officers in the first year.

3. As new people are recruited, alert them to the possibility that some of the current leaders may view

them as intruders. Do not alarm the new persons, but let them know that they may not be welcomed with open arms. Find ways to have the new and current leaders work together on short-term and successful projects.

4. Insist that everyone receive training. Again, this may take two or three years, but it must be a blanket policy that excludes no one. Once it is enacted, power will be more diffuse.

5. Insist that evaluation be a policy for everyone. Again, this will take two or three years to implement. Also, the design of the evaluation will be important. Evaluation, as a positive element in church programming, can introduce significant changes over time.

6. When necessary, use reassignments as a strategy. Reassignment should be introduced as a policy and practice during the training and evaluation processes. It should be used with discretion. Threats to reassign an individual should never be made. When a reassignment is needed, do it.

No strategy is ever foolproof. At the same time, unless the person in charge of volunteers has a plan for dealing with every situation, it will be exceedingly difficult to cope with recruiting, training, assigning, and evaluating volunteers. Churches exist because of volunteer activity. Churches that are vital and express ministry and mission have a volunteer corps that is vital no matter what its special situation may be.

Note: A resource to assist in non-married adult ministries is *The Challenge of Single Adult Ministry* (Valley Forge: Judson Press, 1982). A resource to use with two-worker families is *Ministry with Young Couples* (Nashville: Abingdon Press, 1985). Both of these are by this author.